C000103182

*The Pocket Book of*

# What, When and Who on Earth

*Fascinating facts about Christianity*

# The Pocket Book of
# What, When and Who on Earth

*Fascinating facts about Christianity*

Compiled by George Courtauld

Author of the bestselling phenomenon
**The Pocket Book of Patriotism**

BENE FACTUM PUBLISHING LTD

*For my darling wife Fiona with all my love*

*The Pocket Book of What, When and Who on Earth*
*Compiled by George Courtauld*

First published in 2011 by
Bene Factum Publishing Ltd
PO Box 58122
London
SW8 5WZ

Email: inquiries@bene-factum.co.uk
www.bene-factum.co.uk

ISBN: 978-1-903071-37-3

Text © George Courtauld

The rights of George Courtauld to be identified as the Author of this Work have
been asserted by them in accordance with the Copyright, Designs and Patents Act,
1988.

All rights reserved. This book is sold under the condition that no part of it may be
reproduced, copied, stored in a retrieval system or transmitted in any form or by any
means, electronic, mechanical, photocopying, recording or otherwise without prior
permission in writing of the publisher.

A CIP catalogue record of this is available from the British Library

Cover and book design by Mousemat Design Ltd

Printed and Bound by Clays Ltd, UK.

# INTRODUCTION

As an Englishman, as an Anglican, living in a country steeped in Christianity, it is amazing what I have forgotten or, perhaps, only half remember about my own religion. Our most basic assumptions about right and wrong, our calendar, our very language are all the product of centuries of Christian heritage. Our loveliest buildings, music and literature, our great institutions, our Parliament, even our Head of State are all emphatically Christian and yet it is astonishing what we miss or misunderstand.

Reminding myself of some things and clearing up or discovering others while compiling this book has been not only fascinating but genuinely enlightening.

These are the beliefs, traditions, and words that have sustained some of the greatest engines for good in the world for centuries, and which inspired the noblest heroes and some of the blackest villains, and that still dictate the actions of millions.

What is a sacrament or station of the cross? Why 'Shrove' Tuesday or 'cardinal' sin? What were Protestants protesting about? When did the Pope become infallible? Who were Arius, Ignatius Loyola or George Fox?

Of course, in such a short book I may have neglected essentials and I am sure concentrated too long on things others may think trivial for which I apologise. But, by dividing the material into three main sections, a calendar and timeline, the 'When', a glossary, the 'What', and biographies 'the Who on Earth', I hope the information is easy to find and understand, and that looking up one entry will lead onto others.

Once these were matters of life and death. Some still are.

George Courtauld

# CONTENTS

c.2550 The Great Pyramid of Khufu.

c.1750 The Babylonian Eye for an Eye Law.

c.1650 Jacob and his sons move to Egypt.

c.1250 The Trojan War.

c.1225 Moses given the Ten Commandments.

c.1055-15 The reign of King David.

c.970 The Death of King Solomon of Israel.

c.930 The southern half of Israel splits off to become Judah.

c.776 The first Olympic Games.

c.753 Rome founded by Romulus and Remus.

c.750 The Prophet Isaiah active.

c.720 The people of Israel in Assyria.

c.700 The Prophet Jeremiah active.

604-561 The reign of King Nebuchadnezzar of Babylon.

c.590 The people of Judah in Babylon.

563-483 The Life of Buddha.

551-479 The Life of Confucius.

c.540 The Israelites return from exile.

490 The Greek victory over the Persians at Marathon.

430–404 Athens fights Sparta in the Peloponnesian War.

399 The death of Socrates.

384–332 The life of Aristotle.

356–323 The life of Alexander the Great.

264–146 The Punic Wars between Rome and Carthage.

214 The Great Wall of China completed.

44BC Caesar assassinated.

27BC–14AD Augustus, the first Emperor of Rome.

4, 3 or 0 BC The Birth of Jesus.

| Christianity | Other |
| --- | --- |
| **c.29, 30 or 33AD** The Crucifixion: | |

*"Father forgive them for they know not what they do."*

| Christianity | Other |
| --- | --- |
| | **42** Roman Emperor Caligula assassinated and replaced by Claudius. |
| **c. 49** The First Christian Council in Jerusalem, in which Peter, Paul and James confirm that Gentile Christians do not have to abide by Jewish law. | |
| **c. 50** Paul founds church in Corinth. | |
| **c. 51** Paul debates with Athenian philosophers. | |
| **c. 57** Paul sends his letter to the Galatians. | |
| **c. 58** Paul sends his letter to the Romans. | **58** The Buddhist Ming-Ti becomes Emperor of China. |
| **64** 1st of the 10 great Christian persecutions – by Emperor Nero. | |
| **64** Peter crucified upside down: | |

*"Dominie Quo Vadis?" "Lord where are you going?"*

| Christianity | Other |
| --- | --- |
| **67** Paul beheaded by sword in Rome. | |
| | **70** Romans take and destroy Jerusalem. |
| | **80** The Colosseum completed in Rome. |

| Christianity | Other |
|---|---|
| 84 Christians expelled from Jewish synagogue. | |
| 95 Christians persecuted under Emperor Domitian. | |
| 98–117 Christians persecuted under Emperor Trajan. | |
| | 105 Paper invented in China. |
| | 135 The Romans take Jerusalem. |
| 144 Marcion rejects the Old Testament and is excommunicated. | |
| 177 Christians persecuted under Emperor Marcus Aurelius. | |
| 180–200 St Irenaeus, Bishop of Lyons: | |

*"The glory of God is a man fully alive."*

| Christianity | Other |
|---|---|
| 193–211 Christians persecuted under Emperor Septimus Severus. | |
| | 226 Sassanid dynasty takes control of Persia. |
| 235 Christians persecuted under Emperor Maximinus Thrax. | |
| | 247 The Goths Cross the Danube. |
| 250 Christians persecuted under Emperor Decius. | |
| 258 Christians persecuted under Emperor Valerian. | |
| 272 Christians persecuted under Emperor Aurelian. | |

| Christianity | Other |
|---|---|
| | 297 Emperor Diocletian decrees the destruction of all scientific writing. |
| | c.300 The stirrup invented. |
| 303-5 Christians persecuted under Emperor Diocletian. | |
| 311 Donatist schism. | |
| 312 Constantine places the Christian symbol of the Chi Rho on standards at Battle of Milvian Bridge, winning against overwhelming odds: | |

*"By this sign shall ye conquer."*

| Christianity | Other |
|---|---|
| 313 The two emperors (Constantine and Licinius) meet in Milan and agree toleration of Christianity. The Edict of Milan. | 313 Chin dynasty ends in China |
| 315-40 Eusebius, Bishop of Caesarea. | |
| | 320 In northern India Chandragupta crowned first Gupta Emperor |
| 325 The Council of Nicaea, the first oecumenical church council, condemns the Arian heresy, (that Jesus, the son, was not equal with the Father) proclaiming that the son was *"of the same substance"* as the Father. | |
| 330 Byzantium, renamed Constantinople, celebrated as 'New Rome' with Christian ceremonies. | 331 Constantinople becomes capital of the Roman Empire. |

| Christianity | Other |
| --- | --- |
| 337 Constantine baptized, before he dies. | |
| | 350 Sassanian palace of Feruz–abad built. |
| c.360 St Basil founds the monastic order whose rule followed by Greek and Russian monks. | |
| c.361–3 Julian the Apostate, sole Roman Emperor: | |

*"You have conquered, O Galilean."*

| Christianity | Other |
| --- | --- |
| | 364 The Roman Empire splits in two – East and West. |
| 374 Ambrose, Bishop of Milan. | |
| | 375 The formula for modern soap first recorded. |
| 381 The Council of Constantinople gives the See of Constantinople seniority of honour after Rome. | |
| 382 Pope Damasus and his Council lists the canonical books of the Old and New Testaments. | |
| 384–404 St Jerome translates the Bible into Latin, establishing a standard text called 'The Vulgate'. | |
| 390 The Massacre of Thessalonica. The Emperor, Theodosius I, excommunicated by Ambrose. | 392 Theodosius the Great becomes the last Emperor of both the eastern and western halves of the Roman Empire. |
| 397 'The Confessions' of Saint Augustine, Bishop of Hippo: | |

*"Give me chastity and continency – but not yet."*

| Christianity | Other |
|---|---|
| **400** The British Monk Pelagius denies the importance of original sin. | **c400** Start of recorded history in Japan. |
| | **410** Rome sacked by the Visigoths. |
| **416** The Council of Carthage condemns Pelagius. | |
| **430–60** St Patrick in Ireland. | |
| **431** The Council of Ephesus. Nestorius, Patriarch of Constantinople, condemned for asserting that Christ had two natures, human and divine. | |
| **451** The Council of Chalcedon restates that Christ is one person in 'two natures', human and divine. Unable to accept this, churches in Egypt and Syria separate from Constantinople, eventually forming the Coptic Orthodox Church and Syrian Orthodox Church. | **453** The death of Atilla the Hun. **455** Rome sacked by the Vandals. **469** The Visigoths invade Spain. |
| **496** Clovis, King of the Franks, baptized. | |
| **537** The Haghia Sophia (Church of the Holy Wisdom) completed by Justinian. | **523** The Pagoda of Sung Yueh Temple, Honan, China. |

**c.539** Benedictines founded:
*"We are therefore about to establish a school of the Lord's service in which we hope to introduce nothing harsh or burdensome."*

| Christianity | Other |
|---|---|
| **540–80** Jacob Baradaeus, Bishop of Edessa, founds Monophysite or 'Jacobite' churches. | **542–3** Great global earthquake and Plague |
| **563** Columba and his 12 followers established on Iona. | |
| **590–604** St Gregory the Great, Pope: | |

*"Not Angles but Angels."*

| | |
|---|---|
| **597** Augustine brings Roman Christianity to Kent. | **619–906** The Tang Dynasty, China. |
| **664** The Synod of Whitby settles on the Roman date of Easter, rather than the Celtic. | **625** Mohammed starts reciting the Koran. |
| | **711** The Arabs reach Spain. |
| **726** The Iconoclast controversy erupts. | |
| **731** The Ecclesiastical History of the English People, finished by the Venerable Bede: | |

*"It is better never to begin a good work, than, having begun it, to stop."*

| | |
|---|---|
| | **750** Beowulf. |
| **754** Boniface martyred in Frisia. | **751** The Buddhist 'Diamond Sutra', the first printed book. |
| **775** The See of the Nestorian Patriarch moved to Baghdad. | |

| Christianity | Other |
|---|---|
| 787 The 2nd Council of Nicaea confirms the value of icons. | 788 Work starts on the Great Mosque at Cordoba, Spain. |
| 800 Charlemagne, crowned Holy Roman Emperor, by Pope: | |

*"The voice of the people is the voice of God."* **Charlemagne's secretary, Alcuin.**

| | |
|---|---|
| 815–42 Iconoclasm revival. | |
| 830–65 Anskar preaches in Denmark and Sweden. | 832 Saracens take Sicily. |
| 843 'The Triumph of Orthodoxy'. Icons restored. | 845 Paper money in use in China. |
| 848 Anskar, Archbishop of Bremen. | |
| 863 Communion broken between Patriarch Photius of Constantinople and Pope Nicholas I: The Photion Schism. | |
| 863 Cyril and Methodius, 'The Apostles of the Slavs', in Moravia. Bible translated into Slavonic languages. | 870 Gunpowder invented in China. |
| | 889 Angkor founded. |
| 910 Benedictine Abbey of Cluny founded. | |
| | 911 Rollo the Viking, first Duke of Normandy. |
| | 933 Delhi founded. |
| 961 The Great Lavra founded on Mount Athos. | |

## Christianity

988 Vladimir, Prince of Kiev, baptized.

996-1021 Caliph el-Hakim persecutes Coptic Christians in Egypt.

1009 The Church of the Holy Sepulchre, in Jerusalem, destroyed.

c.1030-1490 Christian reconquest of Spain.

c.1050 The Monastery of the Caves founded in Kiev.

1054 The Catholic and Orthodox churches anathematise each other. The Church splits.

1059 Papal elections become the responsibility of Cardinals.

1060-90 Norman conquest of Muslim Sicily.

1071 The Battle of Manzikert. The Byzantines defeated by Seljuk Turks.

1071 Seljuk Turks take Jerusalem.

1084 St Bruno founds Carthusian Order.

## Other

987 Hugh Capet crowned in France.

992 Venice and Byzantium make their first formal trading agreements.

c.1045 Pi Cheng uses movable type for printing in China.

1066 The Battle of Hastings. The invading Normans defeat the English Saxons.

| Christianity | Other |
|---|---|
| **1093** St Anselm, Archbishop of Canterbury: | |

*"God is that, the greater than which cannot be conceived."*

| | |
|---|---|
| **1096–9** The First Crusade. | |
| **1098** The strict Benedictine monastic order, known as the Cistercians, is founded at Citeaux or Cistercium near Dijon in France. The Grey or White Monks. | |
| **1099** The Crusaders capture Jerusalem. | |
| | **1100** The first Ceremony of Marriage to the Sea performed in Venice. |
| **1113** St Bernard of Clairvaux and 30 followers join Cistercian Abbey at Citeaux: | |

*"You will find something more in woods than in books. Trees and stones will teach you that which you never learn from masters."*

| Christianity | Other |
|---|---|
| | **1116** Bologna University founded. |
| **1119** The first 9 French Knights Templar bind themselves to protect pilgrims. | |
| **1122** The Concordat of Worms. | |
| **1123** The First Lateran Council. | |
| | **1135** Flying buttresses appear in France. |
| **1139** The Second Lateran Council. | |
| | **1140** Arabic numerals adopted in the West. |

| Christianity | Other |
|---|---|
| 1143 Peter the Venerable, Abbot of Cluny, supervises the translation of the Koran into Latin. | |
| 1147-9 The 2$^{nd}$ Crusade. | |
| | 1155 Frederick of Barbarossa proclaimed Holy Roman Emperor. |
| 1170 Archbishop Thomas Becket of Canterbury martyred: | |

*"Will no-one rid me of this turbulent priest?"* **King Henry II.**

| Christianity | Other |
|---|---|
| 1177 The Third Lateran Council. | |
| 1187 Saladin captures Jerusalem. | |
| 1189-92 The 3rd Crusade. | 1192 Yoromito Minamoto proclaimed Shogun of Japan. |
| | 1200 The University of Paris founded. |
| 1201 The 4$^{th}$ Crusade. | |
| 1204 4$^{th}$ Crusaders sack Orthodox Christian Constantinople. Latin kingdom established under Baldwin. | |
| 1208-14 The Albigensian Crusade. | |
| 1209 Franciscans founded by St Francis of Assisi: | |

*"Praise be you, My Lord, with all your creatures, especially Sir Brother Sun, who is the day and through whom you give us light."*

| Christianity | Other |
|---|---|
| 1212 The Children's Crusade. | 1210 China is invaded by Genghis Khan. |

| Christianity | Other |
|---|---|
| 1215 The Fourth Lateran Council. | 1215 The University of Padua founded. |
| 1216 The Dominicans founded. | |
| 1217-21 The 5th Crusade. | |
| | 1224 Genghis Khan leads his Mongols into Europe. |
| 1229 The 6$^{th}$ Crusade: Frederick II negotiates the recovery of Jerusalem. | 1232 The first military use of rockets in China. |
| | 1234 The Chin dynasty brought down by the Mongols. |
| 1244 Jerusalem retaken by Muslims. | |
| 1248-54 The 7$^{th}$ Crusade, lead by Louis IX of France. | 1249 University College, the first Oxford college, founded. |
| 1261 Constantinople regained by Byzantines. | 1250-1570 The Mamelukes rule Egypt. |
| 1267 Thomas Aquinas' 'Summa Theologiae': | |

*"Law: an ordinance of reason for the common good, made by him who has care of the community."*

1270-2 The Last Crusade.

1274 The Orthodox Church rejects the reunion of the Catholic and Orthodox Churches, decreed by the Second Council of Lyon.

| Christianity | Other |
|---|---|
| | 1281 Peterhouse, the first Cambridge college, founded. |
| | 1288–1919 The Ottomans assume power in Turkey. |
| 1291 The Loss of Acre in Syria – the last crusader stronghold. | |
| | 1290 The Jews expelled from England. |
| | c.1300 The longbow in use in Britain. |
| | c.1300 Gunpowder reaches the West. |
| 1302 In 'Unam Sanctam', Pope Boniface VIII declares the universal jurisdiction of the Pope and the dominance of spiritual over secular power. | |
| | 1306 The Jews expelled from France. |
| 1307 Dante's 'Divine Comedy': | |

*"Abandon hope all ye who enter here."*

| Christianity | Other |
|---|---|
| 1309 The Pope leaves Rome for Avignon. | |
| 1312 The Templars brought down. | |
| 1337 The Hesychast Controversy. | 1325 The Aztecs come to power in Mexico. |
| | 1337–1453 The 100 Years War between France and England. |
| c.1340 The Monastery of the Holy Trinity founded outside Moscow. | |
| | 1348 The Black Death in Europe. |
| | 1366 Petrarch's Sonnets. |

| Christianity | Other |
|---|---|
| | 1368-1644 The Ming Dynasty, China. |
| 1374 Geert de Groote founds the Brethren of the Common Life at Deventer in Holland. | |
| 1377 John Wyclif preaches against the Pope, monks and friars and the wealth of the Church: | |

*"This bible is for the government of the people, by the people, and for the people."*

| Christianity | Other |
|---|---|
| 1378-1415 The Great Schism: Rival Popes at Avignon and Rome. | |
| 1387 Florence Radewyns founds Monastery of Windesheim in Holland. | |
| | 1395 The Golden Horde defeated by Tamberlane. |
| 1413 Jan Huss' 'De Ecclesia' demands Church Reform. | 1408 Donatello's 'David'. |
| 1414-18 The Council of Constance: Asserts the superiority of General Councils to Popes and burns Jan Huss at the stake: | |

*"O Holy simplicity."*
*Jan Huss on seeing a peasant lay another faggot on the fire on which he was being burnt at the stake.*

| Christianity | Other |
|---|---|
| 1418 Thomas à Kempis' 'Imitatio Christi'. | |
| | 1420 The Portuguese under Henry the Navigator explore West Africa. |
| | 1430 Van Eyck refines the art of painting in oil. |
| 1440 Ethiopian Church reform by Emperor Zara Jacob. | |

| Christianity | Other |
|---|---|
| 1453 Ottoman Turks take Constantinople. | |
| | 1454 Moveable type used by Gutenberg. |
| 1479 Spanish Inquisition established. | |
| | 1487 Diaz rounds the Cape of Good Hope. |
| 1492 Muslims ejected from Spain. | 1492 Christopher Columbus reaches the West Indies. |
| 1493–4 Pope Alexander VI divides the 'New World' between Spain and Portugal. | |
| 1499 Desiderius Erasmus invited to England. | 1499 John Cabot reaches Newfoundland. |
| | 1503 Leonardo's 'Mona Lisa'. |
| 1506 Work starts on St Peter's in Rome. | |
| | 1516 Macchiavelli's 'The Prince'. |
| 1517 Luther publishes his 95 Theses at Wittenberg. | |
| 1519 Huldrych Zwingli preaches in Zurich. | 1519 Hernando Cortes leads his Spaniards into Mexico. |
| 1521 Luther excommunicated. | 1521 The end of the Aztec Empire. |
| 1521 The Diet of Worms: Luther refuses to recant in front of Emperor Charles V: | |

*"Here I stand. I can do no other. God help me. Amen."*

| Christianity | Other |
|---|---|
| | 1523 Expulsion of Europeans from China. |
| 1524-5 The Peasants' War in Germany. Luther takes the side of 'order' against the peasants. | |
| 1524 The Franciscans established in Mexico. | |
| 1525 William Tyndale's New Testament published: | |

*"If God spare my life, ere many years I will cause a boy that driveth the plough shall know more of the Scripture than thou doest."*

| Christianity | Other |
|---|---|
| 1529 The Diet of Speyer. Lutheran Princes and Cities make a formal 'Protestatio' against the Catholic majority's insistence that religious bodies cannot be deprived of their revenues. | 1528 Coca beans imported into Europe. |
| 1530 The Diet of Augsburg is presented with the Lutheran Confession of Augsburg. | 1530 Death of Babur, founder of the Mogul dynasty in India. |
| 1530 Denmark becomes Lutheran. | |
| 1531 First Bishop in Nicaragua. | |
| 1531 Zumarraga, 1st Archbishop of Mexico, claims the destruction of 500 heathen temples. | |
| 1533-5 Anabaptist Millenarian Commonwealth in Munster. | 1533 The end of the Inca Empire. |

| Christianity | Other |
|---|---|
| **1534** The Act of Supremacy. The Pope's authority in England abolished. | |
| | **1535** The end of the Inca Empire. |
| **1534** The Society of Jesus, the Jesuits, founded. | |

**1535** Sir Thomas More beheaded:
*"They have no lawyers among them, for they consider them as a sort of people, whose profession is to disguise matters."* Utopia.

| Christianity | Other |
|---|---|
| **1535** John Calvin's 'Institutes' (revised 1539) sets out his theological system. | **1535** Cartier reaches the St. Lawrence River. |
| **1537** The Pope insists American Indians are entitled to freedom and property. | |
| **1539** Henry VIII's Great Bible printed. | |
| | **1543** Copernicus's 'De Revolutionibus'. |
| **1545-63** The Council of Trent tries, and fails, to heal the rifts in Christendom caused by the Reformation. | **1547** Ivan the Terrible of Russia adopts the title Tzar. |
| **1549** The First Book of Common Prayer in England. | |
| | **1551** San Marcos University, Lima, Peru, founded. |
| **1552** The Second Book of Common Prayer in England. | |
| **1555-8** England reunited with Rome. | |

| Christianity | Other |
|---|---|

**Christianity**

1555 Protestant theological opponent to Calvin, Michael Servetus, burnt at the stake in Geneva, as a heretic, after being promised safe conduct by Calvin.

1555 The Religious Peace of Augsburg.

1555 Protestant Bishops, Latimer and Ridley, burnt at Oxford:

*"Be of good comfort, Master Ridley, and play the man; we shall this day, by God's grace, light such a candle in England as I trust shall never be put out."*

1556 Protestant Archbishop of Canterbury Cranmer burnt at the stake.

1558 Protestant Elizabeth I assumes the English throne:

*"Twas God the word that spake it*
*He took the bread and brake it*
*And what the word did make it*
*That I believe and take it."*
*Elizabeth's answer to the question of Christ's presence in the sacrament.*

1559 The Index Librorum Prohibitorum (list of prohibited books) instituted by the Inquisition (abolished 1966).

1559 First National Synod of French Reformed Church.

**Other**

1555–1605 Akbar the Great rules India.

1557 The Mosque of Sulieman I, Constantinople, completed.

| Christianity | Other |
|---|---|

**Christianity**

1560 John Knox establishes
reformed church in Scotland:
> *"A man with God is always in the majority."*

1562 The Heidelberg Catechism.

1566 Bullingers' 'Second Helvetic
Confession', summary of
Calvinism, which had a profound
influence on Swiss, French,
Scottish, English, Dutch, German,
Bohemian and Puritan Churches.

1566 Calvinist 'iconoclasts' in
Holland.

1570 The English released from
duty of allegiance to Queen
Elizabeth I by Pope.

1572 The St Bartholomew's Day
Massacre of Protestant Huguenots
in France.

1572 St Teresa in Avila.

1574 Calvinist University at
Leyden founded in Holland.

1577 The Lutheran 'Formula of
Concord'.

1579 The Jesuits reach the Mogul
Court in India.

**Other**

1565 Sir Walter Raleigh introduces
tobacco and potatoes to Britain.

1570 Palladio's 'Four Books of
Architecture'.

1571 The Battle of Lepanto ends
the Turkish threat to Europe from
the sea.

1577-80 Drake's first voyage
around the world.

1588 The Spanish Armada
defeated by the English.

| Christianity | Other |
|---|---|
| **1589** The Church of Russia becomes a Patriarchate. | **1590** First English paper mill at Dartford. |
| **1593** The Wars of Religion in France ended by Henry IV's conversion to Catholicism: | |

*"Paris is worth a mass."*

| Christianity | Other |
|---|---|
| **1593** Sweden becomes Lutheran. | |
| | **1594** Shakespeare's 'Romeo & Juliet'. |
| **1596** The Council of Brest–Litovsk. Orthodox Ukrainians retain their own liturgy but acknowledge Pope's supremacy. | |
| **1598** The Edict of Nantes grants tolerance to French Protestants. | |
| **1599** Synod of Udayamperur: Malabar Christians accept Rome. | |
| | **1600** The East India Company founded. |
| | **1603** James VI of Scotland and I of England unites the two thrones. |
| | **1605** Cervantes 'Don Quixote'. |
| | **1607** Jamestown founded. |
| | **1609** Galileo perfects his telescope. |
| **1611** The Authorised Version or King James Bible published: | |

*"In the beginning God created Heaven and Earth."*

| Christianity | Other |
|---|---|
| **1614** Christianity banned in Japan. | |

| Christianity | Other |
|---|---|
| | |
| | 1618–48 The Thirty Years War. |
| | 1624 Frans Hals's 'Laughing Cavalier'. |
| 1626 Jesuits establish first church in Tibet. | 1626 New Amsterdam (New York) established by the Dutch. |
| | 1632–53 Shah Jahan builds the Taj Mahal. |
| 1633 The Sisters of Charity founded. | |
| | 1635 The Académie Française founded. |
| | 1636 Harvard University founded. |
| 1637 The Shimabara (Christian) Rebellion in Japan. | 1637 The Tulip Crash in Holland. |
| 1640 'Augustinus' by Cornelius Jansen, Bishop of Ypres, published after his death, supporting predestination. | 1642 Rembrandt's 'Night Watch'. |
| | 1643 Louis XIV becomes King of France. |
| | 1644 The Manchus take Peking. The Ch'ing Dynasty established. |
| 1649–60 The Commonwealth in England. Protestant Republic. | 1649 King Charles I executed, London. |
| | 1649 The Russian peasants made serfs. |

| Christianity | Other |
|---|---|
| | 1656 The Jews invited to return to Britain by Oliver Cromwell. |
| 1660 Anglican Church and Crown restored in England. | 1660 The Monarchy restored in Britain. |
| | 1660 The Royal Society founded in London. |
| 1662 The Book of Common Prayer: | |

*"Give us Grace, that, being not like children carried away with every blast of vain doctrine, we may be established in the truth of the Holy Gospel."*

**1666-7** The Schism of Old Believers in Russian Orthodox Church.

**1667** Milton's 'Paradise Lost'.

**1668** George Fox, founder of The Religious Society of Friends, The Quakers, draws up his 'Rule for the Management of Meetings':

*"Walk cheerfully over the world, answering that of God in everyone."*

| | |
|---|---|
| 1673 The Test Act in England requires holders of public or royal office to take oaths of supremacy and allegiance, effectively barring Catholics and many non-Anglicans. Repealed in 1829. | 1674 The Poles elect Jan Sobiewski as King. |
| 1675 Philipp Jacob Spener's 'Pia Desideria', initiates Pietism. | 1677 Racine's 'Phèdre'. |

| Christianity | Other |
|---|---|
| 1678 Richard Simon's 'Histoire critique du Vieux Testament', initiates modern Old Testament criticisms. | |
| 1678 John Bunyan's 'Pilgrim's Progress': | |

*"As I walked through the wilderness of this world..."*

| Christianity | Other |
|---|---|
| | 1679 The last dodo killed. |
| 1682 Pennsylvania founded by the Quaker, William Penn. | |
| | 1683 The Second Ottoman Siege of Vienna. |
| 1685 The Revocation of the Edict of Nantes. | 1687 Isaac Newton's 'Principia Mathematica'. |
| 1692 Imperial tolerance granted to Christianity in China. | 1690 John Locke's 'An Essay concerning Human Understanding'. |
| | 1698 Thomas Savery patents his mine pump. |
| 1701 Society for the Propagation of the Gospel in Foreign Parts founded in England. | 1703 St Petersburg founded by Peter the Great. |
| | 1712 Thomas Newcomen develops the piston engine. |
| 1713 The Papal Bull 'Unigenitus' condemns the Jansenists. | 1714 Gabriel Fahrenheit makes the first mercury thermometer. |

| Christianity | Other |
|---|---|
| 1717 The Anglican Bishop of Bangor preaches before George I on the text 'My Kingdom is not of this World', sparking the Bangorian Controversy. | |
| | 1721 Sir Robert Walpole becomes the first 'Prime Minister' of Britain. |
| 1721 Peter the Great initiates the 'Holy Synod' and abolishes the Moscow Patriarchate, effectively putting the Russian Church under state control. | |
| 1723-6 Christian persecution in China. | |
| | 1725 Vivaldi's 'Four Seasons'. |
| 1725-50 Johann Sebastian Bach's religious compositions. | |
| 1726 'The Great Awakening' begins in USA. | 1734 Voltaire's 'Lettres Philosophiques'. |
| 1738 John Wesley opens first Methodist Chapel in Bristol: | |

*"Men may call me a knave or a fool, a rascal, a scoundrel, and I am content, but they shall never by my consent call me a Bishop."*

| | 1741 Richardson's 'Pamela'. |
|---|---|
| 1742 Handel's 'Messiah': | |

*"Whether I was in my body or out of my body as I wrote it, I know not. God knows."*

| | 1755 The Lisbon Earthquake. |
|---|---|
| | 1756-63 The Seven Years War. |
| 1759 Jesuits expelled from Portugal. | 1762 Rousseau's 'Emile'. |

| Christianity | Other |
|---|---|
| | 1769 Watt's steam engine. |
| | 1770 Botany Bay discovered by Captain Cook. |
| 1773 First Methodist Conference in USA. | |
| 1773 Jesuits suppressed by Pope. | |
| | 1775–81 The American War of Independence. |
| | 1786 Mozart's 'Marriage of Figaro'. |
| 1787 Protestant marriage recognized in France. | |
| | 1789 The French Revolution. |
| 1792 The Baptist Missionary Society founded in London. | |
| 1793–4 State ordered 'dechristianization' in France. | |
| | 1796 Smallpox vaccinations. |
| | 1798 Haydn's 'Creation'. |
| 1799 The Church Missionary Society founded in London. | |
| 1800 'Second Great Awakening' in USA. | |
| 1801 'The Restoration of the Altars'. The Pope's Concordat with Napoleon. | |
| 1801 Catholics persecuted in Korea. | |
| 1804 British and Foreign Bible Society founded. | 1804 Beethoven's 'Eroica Symphony'. |

| Christianity | Other |
|---|---|
| 1807 Protestant missionaries in China. | 1807 Britain abolishes the slave trade. |
| 1808 Baltimore first Catholic 'Metropolitan See' in USA. | |
| 1814 The Consecration of the first Anglican Bishop of Calcutta, the first Anglican Bishop in Asia. | |
| 1814 Samuel Marsden evangelises Maoris in New Zealand. | 1815 The Battle of Waterloo. Napoleon finally defeated. |
| 1816 Elizabeth Fry, the Quaker, forms the Prison Improvement Association: | |

*"Punishment is not for revenge but to reduce crime and reform the criminal."*

| Christianity | Other |
|---|---|
| 1817 Union of German Calvinists and Lutherans. | |
| 1817-67 Robert Moffat begins missionary work in South America. | 1818 Chile declares independence. |
| 1821 Ottomans execute Gregory, Patriarch of Constantinople. | 1821 Peru declares independence. |
| c.1825–35 Persecution of religious orders in Latin America – the Vatican having sided with Spain against the colonies seeking independence. | 1825 The Stockton and Darlington Railway in England. |
| 1829 Roman Catholic and Non-Conformist Emancipation in Britain. | |

| Christianity | Other |
|---|---|
| | 1830 The death of Simon Bolivar. |
| 1832 Start of the Oxford Movement: | |

*"We can believe what we choose. We are answerable for what we choose to believe."*
Cardinal Newman

| Christianity | Other |
|---|---|
| 1836 First Bishop in Australia. | 1833 Slavery abolished in the British Empire. |
| | 1837 The first telegraphic message. |
| 1839 Slavery condemned by Papal Bull. | |
| 1840 Livingstone in Africa. | 1840 The British Penny Post. |
| 1842 First Anglican Bishop of New Zealand. | |
| 1843 Kierkegaard's 'Either-Or'. | |
| 1845 Southern Baptists and Methodists split from American Baptists and Methodists. | |
| 1847 Mormons based at Salt Lake City. | |
| 1848 Pope forced to flee Rome, in the 'Year of Revolutions'. | 1848 Marx and Engel's 'Communist Manifesto'. |
| | 1848 'The Year of Revolutions' in Europe. |
| 1850 Roman Catholic hierarchy re-established in England and Wales. | 1850–65 The Taiping Rebellion in China. |

| Christianity | Other |
|---|---|

**Christianity**

1854 The Immaculate Conception of The Virgin Mary confirmed as an article of faith by Papal Bull.

1858 Bernadette has her visions at Lourdes.

1858 China forced to accept missionaries.

1865 Samuel Crowther consecrated Bishop in Nigeria – the first black Anglican Bishop of Nigeria.

1865 The Pope bans Catholic involvement with Masons.

**Other**

1851 The Great Exhibition in London.

1856 Flaubert's 'Madame Bovary'.

1857–8 The Indian Mutiny.

1859 Darwin's 'Origin of Species'.

1860 Victor Emmanuel proclaimed King of Italy by Garibaldi.

1861 Tzar Alexander II liberates the serfs.

1861–5 The American Civil War.

1864 The International Red Cross founded in Switzerland.

1866 Alfred Nobel invents dynamite.

1867 The typewriter is invented.

| Christianity | Other |
|---|---|
| 1867 76 Anglican Bishops attend the first Lambeth Conference. | |
| | 1869 The Suez Canal opened. |
| 1870 The first Vatican Council: decree of Papal Infallibility. | |

*"A Protestant if he wants advice on any matter can only go to his solicitor."* Disraeli

| Christianity | Other |
|---|---|
| 1871 The Anglican Church in Ireland disestablished. | 1871-90 Bismarck Chancellor of the newly united Germany. |
| | 1872 Tolstoy's 'Anna Karenina'. |
| 1873 Christians no longer, officially, persecuted in Japan. | |
| 1875 The World Alliance of Reformed and Presbyterian Churches formed in Geneva. | |
| 1875 Mary Baker Eddy publishes 'Science and Health'': | |

*"Disease is an experience of so-called mortal mind. It is fear made manifest on the body."*

| Christianity | Other |
|---|---|
| | 1876 Wagner's 'Ring Cycle'. |
| | 1876 Alexander Graham Bell invents the telephone. |
| 1878 The Salvation Army formally takes its name: | |

*"Through Blood and Fire!"*

| Christianity | Other |
|---|---|
| | 1879 Edison demonstrates his electric light. |
| 1884 Protestant missionaries in Korea. | |

## Christianity

1885 The Wallachian, Moldavian and Transylvanian dioceses of the Constantinople Patriarchate combine to become the Romanian Orthodox Church.

1889 Brazilians declare themselves a secular republic.

1896 The Vatican refuses to recognize Anglican orders.

1899 The Gideons founded, to provide Bibles in hotel and hospital bedrooms.

1900 Chinese Christians attacked in Boxer Rebellion.

1906-7 France formally declares the separation of Church and State, allowing the State to appropriate church property.

## Other

1885 Karl Benz builds the first petrol-fuelled car.

1888 Brazil abolishes slavery.

1895 Marconi transmits his wireless messages.

1898 The Curies discover radium.

1903 The Wright brothers achieve the first manned, powered flight.

1904 Freud's 'Psychopathology of Everyday Life'.

1905 Einstein's Theory of Relativity.

| Christianity | Other |
|---|---|
| 1908 The Vatican formally removes Roman Catholicism in Britain and America from the Congregation de Propaganda Fide, the Catholic Church in UK and US recognized as no longer being 'missions' but established churches. | |
| 1908 The South India United Church created by the union of the Presbyterians, Congregationalists and Dutch Reformed Churches in South India. | 1908 Death of Tz'u-hsi, Manchu Dowager Empress of China. |
| 1912 The Australian Inland Mission and Flying Doctor Organization founded. | |
| | 1913 Charlie Chaplin appears in his first film. |
| | 1914–18 The First World War. |
| | 1917 The Russian Revolution. |
| | 1919 The League of Nations. |
| 1920 Anglican church in Wales disestablished. | 1920–33 Prohibition (of alcohol) in the USA. |
| | 1921 Rutherford and Chadwick split the atom. |
| | 1922 Mussolini marches on Rome. |
| | 1924 Lenin dies and Stalin takes power. |

| Christianity | Other |
|---|---|
| | 1926 Baird invents television. |
| 1928 Alfred E Smith, first Catholic candidate for US Presidency. Defeated. | 1928 Sir Alexander Fleming discovers penicillin. |
| 1929 Lateran Treaty, Rome. | 1929 The Wall Street Crash. |
| | 1930 Mohandas (the Mahatma) Gandhi leads the Salt March in India. |
| | 1931 The Japanese invade Manchuria. |
| 1932 The United Methodist Church unites with Wesleyan and Primitive Methodist Churches. | |
| | 1933 Hitler becomes Chancellor of Germany. |
| | 1936-9 The Spanish Civil War. |
| | 1937 Whittle invents the jet engine. |
| | 1939-45 The Second World War. |
| | 1942 Wannsee Conference, Germany, the Nazi party decides on 'The Final Solution', the extermination of all European Jews. |
| 1943 Concordat between Russian Orthodox Church and Stalin. | 1945 The Allies drop Atomic Bombs on Nagasaki and Hiroshima. |
| 1946 Eastern Rite Catholic Church abolished in USSR. | |

| Christianity | Other |
|---|---|
| | 1946 Britain introduces the National Health Service. |
| | 1947 India, Pakistan and Burma gain independence. |
| 1948 World Council of Churches founded. | 1948 The Jewish National Council proclaims the new State of Israel. |
| | 1949 The People's Republic of China established. |
| | 1949 Nato founded. |
| | 1950–3 The Korean War. |
| | 1953 Francis Crick and James Watson identify the structure of DNA. |
| | 1956 The Soviet Invasion of Hungary. |
| | 1957 Ghana gains independence. |
| | 1957 The Treaty of Rome: the founding of the EEC. |

1958 Krushchev initiates further anti-religious measures in USSR:
  *"Whether you like it or not we will bury you. History is on our side."*

1958 Local Roman Catholic priests in China consecrate first Roman Catholic Bishop – against the wishes of the Vatican.

| Christianity | Other |
|---|---|
| 1959 Castro smothers religious freedom in Cuba. | |
| 1960 John Kennedy, first Catholic President of the USA. | 1960 Nigeria gains independence. |

*"Don't buy a single vote more than necessary. I'll be damned if I'm going to pay for a landslide."* President John Kennedy's father

| | |
|---|---|
| 1961 Orthodox Churches join the World Council of Churches, but the Roman Catholic Church does not. | |
| | 1962 The Beatles reach No. 1. |
| | 1963 President John Kennedy assassinated. |
| 1966 All Churches and Temples closed in China. | 1963–75 War in Vietnam. |
| | 1966 The Cultural Revolution enforced in China. |
| | 1967 The 6 Days War between Israel and Egypt. |
| 1968 The Papal Encyclical 'Humanae Vitae' confirms Roman Catholic ban on artificial contraception. | 1968 The Soviet Invasion of Czechoslovakia. |
| 1968 The Baptist Minister, Martin Luther King, assassinated: | |

*"If a man hasn't discovered something he will die for, he isn't fit to live."*

| | |
|---|---|
| | 1969 Man steps on the Moon. |

| Christianity | Other |
|---|---|
| **1970** The Church of North India founded.<br>The Church of Pakistan founded. | |
| **1972** The Congregational Church and Presbytarian Church in England and Wales form the United Reformed Church. | **1973** American forces leave Vietnam. |
| **1978** The Pole Karol Wojtyla is elected Pope John Paul II. | |
| **1979** Churches reopened in China. | **1979** Ronald Reagan elected President of the USA. |
| **1979** Mother Teresa awarded the Nobel Prize: | |

*"I see God in every human being. When I wash the lepers' wounds*
*I feel I am nursing the Lord himself."*

| Christianity | Other |
|---|---|
| | **1980–8** The Iran-Iraq War. |
| **1984** The Chile/Argentinian boundary mediated by the Vatican. | |
| **1986** Desmond Tutu, Anglican Archbishop of Cape Town. | **1986** IBM unveils the first laptop computer. |
| **1988** The Episcopal Church in the US elects a woman bishop. | |
| **1989** Christmas celebrated in old USSR. | **1989** The Tianamen Square Massacre. |
| | **1989** The Berlin Wall torn down. |
| | **1991** The First Gulf War. |

| Christianity | Other |
|---|---|
| | 1991 Sir Tim Berners Lee invents the World Wide Web. |
| | 1993–5 War in Yugoslavia. |
| 1994 The first 32 women ordained as Church of England priests at Bristol Cathedral. | 1994 End of Apartheid. |
| | 1999 The launch of the Euro. |
| 2000 The Millennium. The 2000th anniversary of the birth of Christ. | |
| | 2001 9/11. Al-Quaeda destroy the World Trade Centre. |
| | 2003 The Second Gulf War. |
| 2006 Openly gay, non-celibate Episcopalian priest ordained Bishop of New Hampshire, USA. | |
| | 2008 The Credit Crunch: The American investment bank, Lehman Brothers, collapses causing global recession. |
| 2011 Personal Ordinariate established by the Vatican in England and Wales for groups of Anglican faithful and their Clergy who wish to enter into full communion with the Catholic Church. | 2011 Tsunami and nuclear contamination in Japan |
| | 2011 The Arab Spring |

Advent Sunday:

The Year starts with the first Sunday in Advent. (The Eastern Orthodox Church year begins on St Martin's Day, 11$^{th}$ November.)

Advent is derived from the Latin adventus, arrival. It commemorates the arrival of Jesus: his first coming to redeem the world and looks to his second coming, to judge.

Advent is the four weeks before Christmas from Advent Sunday. Advent Sunday is on St Andrew's Day, 30$^{th}$ November, if a Sunday and if not then the nearest Sunday.

8$^{th}$ December: The Feast of the Immaculate Conception

Celebrating the Roman Catholic Dogma that the Virgin Mary was
*"preserved immaculate from all stain of original sin"*.

21$^{st}$ December: St Thomas the Apostle

25$^{th}$ December: Christmas Day

Celebrating the birth of Christ. This date was fixed by the Church in 440 AD.

26$^{th}$ December: St. Stephen's Day

27$^{th}$ December: St John the Evangelist's Day

28$^{th}$ December: Childermas

Commemorating the Massacre of the Holy Innocents. All the male children under two years ordered to be killed by Herod.

1$^{st}$ January: The Circumcision of Christ

6$^{th}$ January: Epiphany

From the Grk: epiphaneia, an appearance of manifestation.

The manifestation or appearance of Christ to the Gentiles in form of the three Kings. Last of the 12 Days of Christmas.

## 2nd February: Candlemas Day

Formerly the Feast of the Purification of the Virgin Mary, now the Presentation of Our Lord, when all the year's church candles are consecrated.

## Septuagesima Sunday

From the Ltn: seventy.
In round numbers, seventy days before Easter. The third Sunday before Lent.

## 24th February: St Matthias' Day

## Sexagesima Sunday

From the Ltn: sixty.
In round numbers, sixty days before Easter. The second Sunday before Lent.

## Quinquagesima Sunday. Hall Sunday

From the Ltn: fiftieth.
In round numbers, fifty days before Easter. The first day of the week which contains Ash Wednesday.

## Shrovetide. Hall Sunday and Monday and Shrove Tuesday

Hall is a contraction of Hallow, meaning holy. Shrove is derived from the Old English scrifan, to write and means "*to confess, accept penance and receive absolution.*" The time to confess in preparation for Lent.

## Shrove Tuesday. Pancake Day

The day to confess or be 'shriven' before Lent and to use up the last pre-Lent fast supplies in pancakes, etc.

## Ash Wednesday

The first day of Lent, when ashes from the previous Palm Sunday would have been, and in some cases still are, scattered on the heads of penitents.

## Lent

The time of fasting from Ash Wednesday to Easter. From the Old English lencten, lengthen; the Spring when the days lengthen. Fixed at 40 days (it was originally 36) in the early seventh century to match Jesus' time in the Wilderness.

**25th March: The Feast of the Annunciation. Lady Day**
Celebrating the anniversary of the day on which the Angel Gabriel
announced to the Virgin Mary that she would be the mother of Christ.

**1st April: All Fools' Day**

**Laetare Sunday. Mothering Sunday**
Ltn: laetare, rejoice.
The fourth Sunday in Lent, named after the first word sung as the priest
approaches the altar for communion. This was the Sunday on which for
centuries people visited the Mother Church, the oldest or first in the
district, and on which young servants away from home were allowed to
return to their family.

**Care Sunday. Passion Sunday. Judica Sunday**
Care as in suffering; the suffering and passion of Christ.
Judica from the first word if sung in Latin as the priest approaches the altar
for communion.

**Palm Sunday**
The Sunday before Easter, commemorating the day Jesus entered Jerusalem
and palms were laid in his path.

**Holy Week**
The last week of Lent, starting on Palm Sunday.

**Spy Wednesday**
So called by Roman Catholics in Ireland because it is the day when Judas
offered to betray Jesus to the Sanhedrin.

**Maunday Thursday**
The day before Good Friday, from the first words of the chant "*Mandatum
novum do vobis*", "*a new commandment I give you.*" Initiating the ceremony
of the washing of the feet, when Kings and bishops washed the feet of
the poor.

**Good Friday**
The anniversary of the crucifixion.

Holy Saturday. The Great Sabbath

Easter Day
The anniversary of the Resurrection, when Jesus rose from the dead. The date
of Easter was laid down by the Council of Nicaea in 325, as the Sunday
after the first full moon after the Spring Equinox.

25th April: St Mark's Day

Quasimodo Sunday. Low Sunday
The first Sunday after Easter. Low Sunday as opposed to the 'High' Sunday
of Easter. Named after the words from the chant "*Quasi modo geniti
infantes*" "*As newborn babes...*"

1$^{st}$ May: St Philip & St James' Day

Cantate Sunday. Rogation Sunday
The fifth Sunday after Easter. Named after the first words in Latin of the
chant "*Sing to the Lord*". Rogation from the Latin rogare, to ask. The
Sunday before Ascension Day when the 'Litany of Saints' is sung in
procession.

Ascension Day. Holy Thursday
The fortieth Day after Easter, commemorating Jesus' ascent from Earth to
Heaven.

11$^{th}$ June: St Barnabas the Apostle

Whit Sunday
The seventh Sunday after Easter, celebrating the descent of the Holy Ghost
on the day of Pentecost, hence a favourite day for Christening, when
those being baptized wore white, hence White or Whit Sunday.

Trinity Sunday
The Sunday after Whit Sunday. A feast in honour of the Trinity.

Corpus Christi
The Thursday after Trinity Sunday. A festival instituted in 1264 to honour the Blessed Sacrament. A time for the performance of religious dramas and plays.

24th June: St John the Baptist Day

29th June: St Peter's Day

25th July: St James the Apostle

15th August: The Feast of the Assumption
Commemorating the Assumption of the Virgin Mary's body into Heaven.

24th August: St Bartholomew the Apostle

29th September: Michaelmas Day
The Festival of St Michael and all the Angels.

1st October, or the nearest Sunday: Harvest Festival
The first Harvest Thanksgiving was celebrated in Cornwall in 1843 and the practice gradually spread throughout the Church of England.

31st October: All Hallows' Eve. Halloween
The Eve of All Saints' Day, hallow meaning holy, as in Holy Ones, Saints.

1st November: All Saints' Day
In celebration of All the Saints.

2nd November: All Souls' Day

**Aaron**
The first Jewish priest, brother of
Moses.

**Abaddon**
The Angel of the Bottomless Pit.

**Abednego**
Companion of David, Shadrach
and Meshach. Captured by
Nebuchadnezzar the Babylonian.

**Abel**
Son of Adam and Eve. Shepherd.
Brother to Cain, by whom he was
murdered.

**Abraham**
Patriarch. Originally named Abram,
renamed Abraham, meaning Father
of many nations, when God told
him he would be the father of his
chosen people, Israel. Husband of
Sarah, by whom he had Isaac. Father
of Ishmael, the father of the Arabs,
by Sarah's handmaiden Hagar.

**Absalom**
Beautiful third son of King David
who, after rebelling against his
father, was killed by his father's
general Joab while snagged in the
branches of a tree. Leading to
'David's Lament': *"Absalom, my son,
my son Absalom! Would God I had died
for thee! O Absalom my son, my son!"*

**Adam**
The first man, husband of Eve,
author of original sin. Father of
Cain, Abel and Seth.

**St Agatha**
Horribly martyred in Sicily around
250, St Agatha is sometimes
depicted carrying her severed
breasts on a plate. Her Feast Day is
5$^{th}$ February.

**St Agnes**
A 12 year old Christian girl
ordered to marry a Roman pagan.
She refused and was sent to a
brothel. The first man who saw her
naked went blind and she was
beheaded in 305. Her symbol is a
lamb. Saint's Day 21$^{st}$ January.

**Ahitophel**
King David's treacherous
counsellor who supported his son,
Absalom.

**Aholah & Aholibah**
Prostitutes used by Ezekiel to
represent the temptation of false
religions.

**St Alban**
The first Christian martyred in
Britain. Decapitated in 305 at
Verulamium (now St Albans) for
protecting a Christian priest. His

Anglican feast day is on the 17th June (Catholic on 22nd). A monastery in his name was built by Offa in 795.

## Ammann, Jacob
An ultra-conservative who split away from the Mennonites in 1690 and settled in America with his followers, now known as the Amish.

## St Ambrose, 339-397
Despite not then yet having been Christened, made Bishop of Milan in 384 through public acclaim. A fearless lawyer who successfully opposed the Arian heresy, he is sometimes depicted with the whip with which he drove them from Italy. He condemned the Emperor for a massacre by soldiers and shamed him into public penance. Saint's Day 7th December.

## St Andrew
Brother of St Peter, fisherman and Apostle. Crucified 70AD on a saltire, to which he was tied, not nailed, to prolong his agony. He simply continued to preach from the cross. Patron saint of Scotland and Russia. Saint's Day 30th November.

## The Anti Christ
Also called the Man of Sin, destined to arrive at the end of the world before the return of Christ.

Variously identified through the ages as The Roman Empire, many Emperors, Popes and Rulers.

## St Anthony The Great or of Egypt, 251-356
The father of Christian Monasticism. Despite his wealthy family and upbringing, Anthony chose a life of self-denial and austerity, first in a tomb, where he was tormented and tempted by demons, and then in an empty fort. Saint's Day 17th January.

## St Anthony of Padua, 1194-1231
Portuguese nobleman who became a Franciscan and mesmerising roving preacher. He lambasted tyranny and urged care for the poor, even the fish in the River Brenta, raising their heads out of the water to listen. He was also a famous miracle worker. Saint's Day 13th June.

## Ariel
Hebrew name meaning 'Lion of God' and applied to Jerusalem in Isaiah.

## Arius
A Presbyter of the Church of Alexandria in the 4th century, who denied that Jesus was 'of the same substance' as the Father. He claimed that Jesus was not human, though flesh and blood, but in fact

divine, though separate from and inferior to the Father. He and his followers were condemned as Heretics at the Council of Nicaea in 325.

**Arminius (Jacob Hermansen 1560-1609)**
Anti-Calvinist, Professor and founder of Arminians, who believed that faith and repentance were all that was necessary for eternal life.

**Asaph**
One of King David's musicians.

**St Athanasius, 298-373**
One of the four principal Doctors of the Eastern Church, after whom the Athanasian Creed is named. The 20th Bishop of Alexandria from 328 to 373.
*"And in this Trinity none is afore, or after other; none is greater, or less than another; but the whole three persons are co-eternal together: and co-equal."*

**St Augustine (of Canterbury)**
The Apostle of England and First Archbishop of Canterbury. Sent by Gregory the Great as missionary to England with 40 monks. Based himself in Canterbury in 597 and reintroduced international Roman Christianity to Britain, re-establishing Britain's connection with Europe. He died in 604.

**St Augustine of Hippo (modern Annaba in Algeria), 354-430**
Principal Doctor of the Latin Church. Christened by St Ambrose in 386. He savaged contemporary heretics and has himself been attacked for his teaching on sex and predestination. He wrote 'The City of God' and 'Confessions' and contributed enormously to Christian thought on the Trinity, Creation, Grace, the sacraments and the Church.

**Baal**
Canaanite word for God, Lord, master and owner.

**Mary Baker Eddy, 1821-1910**
Founder of Christian Science, who published 'Science and Health' in 1875 and married Mr Eddy, a talented administrator and organizer, in 1879.

**Balaam**
A false prophet.

**Balthasar**
One of The Three Kings. See Kings.

**Barabas**
Criminal chosen for pardon and release by the crowd when Pontius Pilate offered them the chance to choose him or Jesus.

**Baradaeus, Jacob**
Sixth century Bishop of Adessa
who founded a sect of Syrian and
Egyptian Monophysite Christians.

**St Barbara**
The patron saint of Artillery,
Canons and Arsenals and those
afraid of thunder and lightning.
Betrayed by her pagan father for
becoming a Christian, he was
struck by lightning as he raised the
sword to behead her.

**St Barnabas**
St Paul's adjutant on his mission to
the Gentiles (non-Jews).
Symbolized by a rake, as his Saint's
day, 11th June, fell in harvest time.

**St Bartholomew/called
Nathaniel in John's Gospel**
Flayed alive for refusing to worship
the Emperor on 24th August (now
his Saint's Day), AD 44.
Accordingly symbolized by a knife.
Now patron saint of butchers and
plastic surgeons.

**St Basil the Great, c329–379**
From a family of saints, Basil had
an exceptional education with
both the Emperor Julian and fellow
Doctor of the Eastern Church, St
Gregory Naziansen, as classmates.
He wrote the rules for the
monasticism of the Eastern
Orthodox Church and was a great

champion of pastoral care and
critic of the Arian heresy.

**Bathia**
Pharoah's daughter who found
Moses.

**Bathsheba**
The wife of Uriah the Hittite,
desired by King David, resulting in
his effective murder of her
husband. Mother of King
Solomon.

**The Venerable Bede, c 673–735**
Northern British monk and Saint
who wrote 40 books including the
History of the English Church and
People, for which he has been
dubbed "the Father of British
history".

**Beelzebub**
Or Baalzebul or Baal zebub. Lord
of the Flies. The God of Ekron in
Kings and The Prince of the Devils
in Mark and Luke.

**Belphegor**
Or Baal-Peor, God of the Moabites
in Shithim, whose followers
indulged in orgies, tempting the
Israelites.

**Belshazzar**
Son of King Nebuchadnezzar of
Babylon, who replaced him as
King and drank from the gold and

silver vessels from the Temple of Jerusalem. By translating the words in his dream, Daniel predicted his downfall and replacement by Darius the Mede.

St Benedict (of Nursia), c480–c553
Founder of the Benedictines or Black Monks based in Monte Casino, and the writer of the Rule of Saint Benedict, an engine for European stability and civilisation at a time of anarchy and chaos.

Benjamin
The youngest and favourite son of Jacob, framed by Joseph.

St Bernard, 1090–1155
The Mellifluous Doctor. Hugely wise and able Cistercian Abbot of Clairvaux.

St Boniface, 680–754
The Saxon Wynfrith from Wessex known as the Apostle of Germany.

General William Booth, 1829–1912
Methodist Preacher of outstanding personal sanctity, who broke with the Methodists and founded the Salvation Army, formally given that name in 1878.

St Brandon/Brendon, 484–579
Founder of the Abbey of Clonfert.

Legend is that the 'Rule of St Brandon' was dictated to him by an Angel and he spent seven years searching for the 'Land of the Saints', the Isle of St Brendon off the West Coast of Ireland.

Bunyan, John, 1628–1688
Nonconformist preacher who wrote the great Christian allegory, 'Pilgrims' Progress', on release from prison.

Caedmon, c600–680?
'The father of English song'. Commanded by an Angel to 'Sing the Creation'.

Cain
Son of Adam and Eve and brother of Abel. A 'tiller of the ground', he murdered his brother Abel, when Abel's sacrifice was accepted by God above his own. God cursed Cain to wander the earth bearing 'the mark of Cain'. *"Am I my brother's keeper?"* Genesis 4. 9.

Caiphas
The Jewish High Priest at the time of the Crucifixion.

Calvin, John, 1509–1564
Great Protestant Reformer who in 'Institutio Religious Christianae' in 1536 insisted on the sole authority of the Holy Ghost and the Bible, that through Predestination God

had already chosen the saved or 'elect' so that there was no salvation but through God, and that Church communities should enforce religious discipline.

Caspar
One of The Three Kings. See Kings.

St Catherine
Virgin Alexandrian noblewoman who lambasted the Emperor Maximinus for his persecution of Christians. He challenged her to debate with 50 pagan philosophers in 310, many of whom she converted. She then converted the Empress when she came to visit her in prison. She was put on a bladed killing wheel, which collapsed and was so beheaded, bleeding milk not blood. She consequently became patron saints of nursemaids, wheelwrights and philosophers. Feast Day 25th November.

St Cecilia
Blind patron saint of music, from Rome. Martyred around 200, supposed to have invented the organ. Feast day 22nd November.

Chamuel or Chemuel
The Angel who wrestled with Jacob and strengthened Jesus during the Agony in the Garden.

St Christopher
Patron Saint of travellers, who once carried Jesus across a river, hence his name which means Christ carrier. He preached in Lycia and was martyred by beheading. According to legend, anyone looking on an image of St Christopher will not die that day.

St Columba, c521-597
Irish monk of royal blood who founded the Monastery at Derry in 546 and at Durrow and Kells. In 563 he and 12 followers founded a monastery at Iona, from which he converted many in Scotland, including the King of the Northern Picts. His name means dove and he died in the year St Augustine came to England. Saint's Day 6th June.

Constantine the Great
Emperor who put the Chi Rho on his standards in 312 and convinced his fellow Emperor, Licinius, to grant tolerance to Christians in 313. Renamed Byzantium Constantinople and was baptized before he died in 337.

Cranmer, Thomas, 1489-1556
Archbishop of Canterbury, Creator of The Book of Common Prayer and Protestant Martyr.

## St Crispin, 827-869

One of two brothers from Rome who went to France in c300 and maintained themselves by shoemaking. Crepis is Greek for shoe. The Battle of Agincourt took place on St Crispin's Day, 25 October.

## St Cyril

Constantine, or Cyril, and his brother Methodius, were known as the Apostles to the Slavs. Cyril invented the Cyrillic alphabet. Saint's Day 14th February in the Western Church, 11th May in the Eastern Church.

## Dagon

Half-man, half-fish God of the Philistines in Canaan.

## Daniel

Royal Israelite, captured by King Nebuchadnezzar of Babylon, who won favour by defying his captors and following God's laws. He was thrown into the Lions' den by King Darius the Mede, but survived.

## Dante Alighieri, 1265-1321

Florentine poet who settled in Ravenna and wrote the 'Divine Comedy' in 1307.

## David, 1085 BC –

The youngest son of Jesse, who slew Goliath and replaced Saul as King of Israel. He made Jerusalem his capital, recovered the Ark of the Covenant, but engineered the death of Uriah the Hittite so he could take his wife, Bathsheba, and so was rebuked by the Prophet Nathan. Nevertheless they had a child, King Solomon. A skilled harpist; many of the Psalms are attributed to him.

## St David

Patron saint of Wales. Sixth century principal Bishop of South Wales, who allegedly visited Jerusalem and was an uncle of King Arthur. Saint's Day 1st March.

## Delilah

Samson's betrayer.

## St Denys or Dionysus

Apostle to the Gauls and patron saint of France until the French Revolution. After his decapitation in 272, he is reputed to have carried his own head the two miles to where his cathedral would be built. Saint's Day 9th October.

## Dives

The rich man in the parable of the rich man in Luke.

## St Dominic, 1170-1221

Founder of the Dominican Order of Preaching Friars. His opposition to the Albigenisan heretics earned him the role of Inquisitor General.

**Donatus**
Fourth century Numidian Bishop, who believed only holy people should be in the church and that sinners should be banned or expelled. His followers, the Donatists, were condemned by St Augustine of Hippo.

**Dorcas**
The woman St Peter raised from the dead.

**Dysmas**
The 'penitent thief', who recognized Jesus on the cross. Sometimes also called Dimas or Titus.

**Ebenezar**
Hebrew name for 'Stone of Help'. Became increasingly identified with Nonconformists in 17$^{th}$ & 18$^{th}$ centuries.

**St Edmund, 855-870**
King of East Anglia. One time patron saint of England. Bound to a tree and shot with arrows because he refused to become a puppet of the Vikings. His body, miraculously preserved, was buried at the Abbey of Bury St Edmunds. Feast Day 20th November.

**Elijah**
Prophet from Tishbe in Gilead, scourge of King Ahab and Jezebel, who killed 450 prophets of Baal at the River Kishon and found God in *"a still small voice."* Taken up to Heaven in a whirlwind and appeared with Jesus at the Transfiguration.

**Elisha**
Prophet, son of Shaphat, from Abel Meholah, who was anointed by Elijah as his successor *"the chariot of Israel and the horsemen thereof."*

**Elohim/Eloah**
The plural and singular Hebrew words for God.

**Erasmus, Desiderius, 1466-1536**
Mellow Dutch scholar, who had a profound influence on contemporary thinking in Europe and also at Oxford and Cambridge.

**Esau**
Jacob's older twin brother, son of Isaac and Rebekah. A hunter and his father's favourite, much hairier than his brother, through which he was cheated of his father's blessing.

**Eve**
Hebrew: Havvah, life or life-giving
The first woman, created from Adam's rib, mother of Cain, Abel and Seth, who prompted Adam into tasting the Apple from the Tree of the Knowledge of Good and Evil, as she had done, resulting in Man's expulsion from Paradise.

*"This new bone of my bones, and flesh of my flesh: she shall be called Woman, because she was taken out of Man."*

Ezekiel
Optimistic prophet to the Jews in exile in Babylon, where they were taken in 597 BC.

St Francis of Assisi, 1181–1226
Founder of Franciscan order of Friars. He used his inheritance to repair a local church and then set off preaching, supporting himself by begging. He insisted on extreme poverty and obedience to the Pope and Bishops. His joy, his followers were called the Lord's Minstrels as they were always singing, his wisdom and compassion make him much loved. *"What a man is in the sight of God, so much he is and no more."*

Fox, George, 1624–1691
English founder of the Society of Friends, now called The Quakers. *"All bloody principles and practices, we, as to our own particulars, do utterly deny …. and this is our testimony to the whole world."*

St Gabriel
The Archangel who explained visions to Daniel, announced the future birth of John the Baptist to his father, Zacharias, and appeared to The Virgin Mary in the

Annunciation. The name means God is my Strength in Hebrew. *"Hail thou that Art Highly favoured, the Lord is with thee: blessed art thou among women."*

St George
A Roman officer martyred at Lydda around 300AD, or the Arian Bishop of Alexandria, George of Cappadocia. He came to the aid of British Crusaders at Antioch 1098 and they adopted his red cross on a white background as their flag. Edward III made him patron saint of England. His feast day is 23rd April.

Gestas
The impenitent thief, who scorned Jesus on the cross.

St Gregory the Great, 540–604
Pope, Doctor of the Church, Apostle of England, Compassionate, Brilliant Administrator and Reformer. His interest in church ritual and music is still evident in plainsong or the Gregorian Chant. It was he who despatched St Augustine to England.

St Gregory Naziansen, the Theologian
One of the three Holy Hierarchs of the Eastern Church, he ran away when first called to be a priest and wrote on the nature of God and the priesthood.

## Ham
Son of Noah and father of the Canaanites. Cursed by Noah for seeing him drunk and naked.

## Herod Antipas, 20 BC – 39 AD
Tetrarch (Ruler of a quarter) of Galilee and Perea, from 4 AD – 39 AD. Married to Herodias, the wife of his brother, for which he was criticised by John the Baptist, whom he eventually had executed. Pilate handed over Jesus to Herod Antipas for his opinion, but he sent him back.

## Herod Agrippa, 10 BC – 44 AD
King Herod in Acts of the Apostles. Reigned from 41 AD – 44 AD. Grandson of Herod the Great. He tried to win favour with the Jews by persecuting Christians.

## Herod the Great, 73 BC – 4 AD
King of Judea, from 37 BC to 4 AD, who ordered the Massacre of the Innocents.

## St Hubert
Patron saint of Huntsmen.

## St Hugh, 1140-1200
The founder of the first Carthusian Monastery in England. From Burgundy.

## Huss, Jan, 1369-1415
Dean of Philosophy in Prague, who promoted the ideas of John Wycliff.

## St Ignatius
Was the child Jesus *"set in the midst of his disciples as an example"*. Made Bishop of Antioch by St Peter. Thrown to the wild Beasts in Rome by Trajan in 107. Feast Day 17th October.

## Isaac
Son of Abraham and Sarah, bound and laid on a pile of wood in preparation for sacrifice, but reprieved by God at the last minute. Husband of Rebekah, father of the twins, Jacob and Esau.

## Isaiah
One of the four 'Great Prophets' of the Old Testament, his name means God is Salvation and much of his teaching relates to the Messiah, both as a King and a suffering servant. Active in the second half of the eighth century BC, Jewish legend relates that he was eventually sawn in half on the orders of the Jewish King Manasseh.
*"Behold a Virgin shall conceive, and bear a son, and shall call his name Immanuel."* Isaiah 7. 14.

## Ishmael
Son of Abraham and his concubine Hagar, handmaid of Sarah. Hagar was driven into the wilderness by Sarah before Ishmael was born. Father of the Arabs.

Israel
See Jacob.

Jacob
Younger twin son of Isaac and
Rebekah, born clasping his older
brother Esau's heel. Jacob means
'he takes by the heel' or 'he
replaces'. He stole his brother
Esau's birthright, then fled.
He wrestled with God and was
given a new name, Israel, which
means either 'the one who strives
with God' or 'God strives'. He
fathered twelve sons, including
Joseph, who themselves fathered
the 12 tribes of Israel. At the
invitation of his son, Joseph, he and
his sons and their livestock moved
to Egypt.

St James the Great
Son of Zebedee and brother of St
John. Preached in Spain, of which
he is patron saint, and where his
relics are at the Church of Santiago
de Compostela, and which became
the third most important site of
Christian pilgrimage after Jerusalem
and Rome. Hence his symbol is a
scallop shell, used by pilgrims to
scoop drinking water. He was the
first Apostle to be martyred, in
44AD, by the sword. Saint's Day
25th July, Western Church, 30th
April, Eastern Church.

St. James the Less
One of the brothers of Jesus who
may have written the Epistle of St
James and may have been the first
Bishop of Jerusalem. He was
martyred by being stoned and sawn
in two.

Jehu
The son of Nimshi, who drove
'furiously' in II Kings.

JHVH
See Jehovah on page 87 in
Glossary.

Jeremiah
Miserable, outcast prophet, author
not only of the Book of his name
but also Kings I and II and the
Book of Lamentations. He urged
repentance on Israel and was
ignored. Eventually taken to Egypt
and stoned.
*"Can the Ethiopian change his skin,
or the leopard his spots? Then may ye
also be good, that are accustomed to do
evil."* Jeremiah 13. 23.

Jeroboam
'A mighty man of valour' who
'made Israel to sin' I Kings, 11.

## St Jerome, 341-420

A scholar from Rome, he produced the standard Latin text of the Bible: the Vulgate. He founded a monastery in Bethlehem where he removed a thorn from a lion's paw, which followed him around ever after.

*"Consummatum est." "It is finished."*
The Vulgate. John 19. 30.

## Jesse

Father of King David.

## Jesus

From the same root as Isaiah, Hosea and Joshua, meaning 'God is salvation'.
The Son of God. The son of Mary. The Messiah. See page 112–114.

## Jezebel

Wife of Ahab, King of Israel, II Kings, 9.

## St Joachim

Husband of St Anne, father of the Virgin Mary.

## Job

Patient sufferer at God's hands, who finally cracks, but because of his love of God is restored to wealth, health and happiness.

## St John The Evangelist or The Divine

From the Hebrew Jochanan, meaning God is gracious. Traditionally the 'Beloved Disciple' and author of the fourth Gospel, three Epistles and the Book of Revelations. Son of Zebedee and brother of James the Great, fishermen. He is supposed to have escorted The Virgin Mary to Ephesus, been plunged into boiling oil during the persecution of Domitian, but survived, and been banished to the Isle of Patmos, where he wrote the Book of Revelations.

## St John Chrysostom, 347-407

Bishop of Constantinople. One of the three Holy Hierarchs and Doctor of the Eastern Church. A mesmerizing preacher, Chrysostom means golden-tongued.

## St John the Baptist

Son of Zacharias and Elizabeth, cousin of The Virgin Mary. The prophesized herald of the coming Messiah, he baptized those he persuaded to turn back to God in the River Jordan. He baptized Jesus. His severed head was given by King Herod to his stepdaughter, Salomé, as a reward for her dancing.

## Jonah

Prophet who fled by boat to Tarshish *"to flee from the presence of the Lord"* and avoid God's order to rebuke Nineveh for its wickedness. Thrown from the boat, he was swallowed by a whale, in which he spent three days and nights, until he was vomited onto dry land and persuaded Nineveh to mend its ways.

## Joseph
The second youngest of the twelve sons of Jacob who had the famous many-coloured coat. Interpreter of Pharoah's dreams, Governor of Egypt and responsible for Jacob and all his sons moving to Egypt.

## St Joseph
Carpenter husband of the Virgin Mary. Patron saint of carpenters.

## Joseph of Arimathea
Jewish believer in Jesus, who gave up his own tomb for Jesus. According to legend, after 12 years in prison and his release by Vespasian in the year 63, he came to England with the Grail and Spear and founded Glastonbury

## Joshua
Replaced Moses as leader of the Israelites and took them over the River Jordan into the Promised Land, where he took Jericho.

## Judas Iscariot
Iscariot has been translated as 'man of Kerioth', in which case Judas was the only disciple not from Galilee. He was the group treasurer and betrayed Jesus for 30 pieces of silver. Matthew says Judas hanged himself after the crucifixion.

## St Jude
Apostle, brother of James, brother of Jesus. Martyred in Persia with St Simon on 28th October.

## Julian the Apostate, 361-3
Roman Emperor and nephew of Constantine, who rejected Christianity aged 20 and tried to restore paganism.

## St Kentigern/St Mungo
See St Mungo

## St Kevin
6th Century Irish saint who, being pestered by a girl called Kathleen, flogged her with nettles, and may even have hurled her from a cliff. Her ghost haunted him until his death. Roasted on a gridiron.

## The Three Kings
Wise men or Magi from the 'rising sun', translated as East, who visited the Holy Family having followed a star. They were the first non-Jews to recognise Jesus as Christ and are mentioned only in Matthew's Gospel. Assumed to be three by the Western Church because there were three gifts; The Eastern Church maintain there were twelve magi. The three gifts are said to represent:

Gold for Kingship
Frankincense for Divinity
Myrrh for Death
Their names are traditionally
Caspar, Melchior and Balthasar.
Their relics are at Cologne.

St Lawrence
San Lorenzo. Roman deacon.
Roasted alive on an iron grill by
the Emperor Valerian in 258. When
the Emperor demanded the
treasures of the Church, he offered
him the poor and sick of Rome.

Longinus/Longus
The centurion who pierced the
side of Christ on the cross.

Lot
Abraham's nephew who lived in
Sodom and whose wife turned
into a pillar of salt. His sons, by his
own daughters, were the fathers of
the Moabites and Ammonites.

St Ignatius Loyola, 1491-1556
Founder of the Jesuits, the Society
of Jesus. Nobleman, wounded at
the Siege of Pamplona in 1521, he
left the army and dedicated himself
to The Virgin Mary.

Lucifer (Ltn: Light bringer)
Satan, Angel driven out of heaven
for his pride.

St Lucy
Patron saint of those with disease of
the eyes. When pestered by a Duke,
who raved about her eyes, she
plucked them out and said 'leave
me to God'. Martyred in c 300.

St Luke the Evangelist
Patron saint of artists and doctors.
Saint's Day 18th October.

Martin Luther 1483-1546
The foremost figure of the
Reformation, Augustinian Professor
of Scripture at Wittenberg
University, who underwent a
religious inspiration called the
'Tower Experience'. Horrified by
an earlier visit to Rome and the sale
of indulgences to raise money for St
Peter's in Rome, he nailed his "95
Theses" to the door of Wittenberg
Church in 1517. He and his
writings were condemned by Papal
Bull in 1520, but far from recanting
he in fact produced his great
German translation of the Bible.

St Mark the Evangelist
Gospel writer and Bishop who
died in prison in 68AD.
Traditionally the man who ran
away naked when the soldiers
came to arrest Jesus. Saint's Day
25th April.

St Martha
Supposed sister of Lazarus and

Mary Magdalene. Patron saint of Good housewives. Feast Day 29<sup>th</sup> July.

**St Martin**
Patron saint of publicans and drunks, Bishop of Tours in 371, died c 400.

**The Virgin Mary**
The mother of Christ. Saint Mary. Daughter of Joachim and Anne. Wife of Joseph (see page 123).

**St Mary Magdalene**
Patron saint of penitents. Feast day 22 July. Cleansed of seven demons by Jesus as recorded in Luke and Mark. She was present at Jesus' crucifixion and burial, and, according to John and Mark, the first person to see Jesus after his Resurrection.

**St Matthew the Evangelist**
Publican, tax collector for the Romans. Evangelist and Apostle. Converted Ethiopia, where he was martyred.

**St Matthias**
Follower of Jesus, chosen by lot to replace Judas Iscariot as the twelfth Apostle.

**Melchior**
One of the three kings.

**Menno, Simon, 1492-1511**
Anabaptist and pacifist, whose followers, the Mennonites, rejected the Christening of children, clergy and the holding of all 'offices of state'. His following spread from Friesland to Scotland, Germany and America.

**Meshach**
One of the companions of Daniel, captured by Nebuchadnezzar.

**St Michael**
Leader of the Archangels and God's Armies, who casts Satan down to Earth in Revelations 12 and whose name means 'Who is like God' in Hebrew.

**Milton, John, 1608-1674**
Puritan poet, parliamentarian and author of 'Paradise Lost' and 'Paradise Regained'. *"Give me liberty to know, to utter, and to argue freely according to conscience, above all liberties."*

**More, Sir Thomas, 1478-1535**
English lawyer, writer and Lord Chancellor during the reign of Henry VIII who was martyred for his opposition to his monarch's assumption of the Headship of the Church of England. Decapitated in 1535. *"This hath not offended the King,"* on clearing his beard from the block.

## Moloch
From the Hebrew: Molech, King.
God of the Ammonites.

## Moses
Frightened by the growth in the number of Israelites in Egypt, the Pharoah ordered that all Israelite boy babies be thrown into the Nile. Moses' mother placed Moses in a papyrus basket in the river where he was discovered by Pharoah's daughter, who rescued him. Moses means 'I drew him from the water'. God appeared to Moses and assured him that the Israelites would be free and reach the Promised Land. Moses extorted the release of the Israelites from Pharoah by inflicting a number of plagues on the Egyptians. He led the Jews on the Exodus, parted the Red Sea and received the Ten Commandments but never entered the Promised Land himself.

## St Mungo/St Kentigern
From Gaelic: Mungo, dearest. Patron saint of Glasgow, Apostle of the North and founder of Glasgow Cathedral.

## Nathan
The prophet who condemned King David for engineering the death of his lover's husband, Uriah the Hittite.

## Nebuchadnezzar, 604–561BC
The Great King of Babylon, responsible for the Hanging Gardens and much else. Misspelling of Nebuchandrezzar, meaning 'Nebo protects the crown'. Nebo or Nabu was the Babylonian God of Wisdom, the legendary creator of writing.

## St Nicholas
Santa Claus or Father Christmas. Bishop of Lycia, present at the Council of Nicaea in 325, where he is supposed to have slugged Arius. Patron saint of Russia, clerks, pawnbrokers and little boys. His sign of three golden balls representing the three dowries he provided to three women to save them from prostitution. He restored three boys to life after they had been butchered and salted in preparation for making into bacon. Feast Day 6th December.

## Noah
Descendant of Adam and Eve's third son, Seth. When God decided to drown mankind because of its wickedness, Noah, as a righteous man, was entrusted to build an ark to save the animals.

## St Patrick, 373–463
Patron Saint of Ireland, who converted the country to Christianity and banished snakes.

Originally called Sucat but dubbed the Patrician or Patrick when captured and sold as a slave to Miliuc, a chief of Antrim. Escaped and studied under Martin of Tours before converting Ulster.

*"Christ beside me,*
*Christ before me,*
*Christ behind me,*
*Christ within me,*
*Christ beneath me,*
*Christ above me."*
The Breastplate of St Patrick.

St Paul the Apostle to the Gentiles, 10AD-66AD
One of the Princes of the Apostles, the other is St Peter, Apostle to the Jews. Born in Tarsus a Roman citizen, he became a Pharisee, loathed and persecuted Christians and participated in the stoning of St Stephen, when he looked after the executioners' cloaks. He was originally called Saul. Struck blind by a vision of Christ on his way to Damascus, he was cured when Ananias laid his hands on him. On converting Sergius Paulus, he changed his own name to Paul. After much missionary work, he was beheaded in Rome during the persecutions of Nero.

St Paul the Hermit
Egyptian hermit. Died in 341 at a great age and his grave was supposed to have been dug by two lions.

Pelagius
British monk condemned as a heretic in 417 for challenging the importance of original sin. Pelagius is the Latin version of the Welsh Morgan, the sea.

St Peter, the Apostle to the Jews
One of the Princes of the Apostles, originally called Simon, he was the brother of St Andrew. When Peter told Jesus that he was the Messiah, Jesus said, *"You are Peter (Stone) and on this rock I will build my church."* In John's Gospel the Aramaic word for stone, Cephas, is used rather than the Greek, Peter. He was the first Apostle to whom Jesus appeared after the resurrection. He was crucified upside down in Rome in 65AD. St Peter's in Rome is built on his tomb. He was the first Pope and is the patron saint of fishermen.

Peter the Hermit, 1050-1115
Instigator of the 1st Crusade which took Jerusalem.

Pontius Pilate
The fifth Prefect of the Roman province of Judea, from AD 26-36. The judge at Jesus' trial.

St Raphael
Leader of the Guardian Angels, the Powers, Raphael means God is my health in Hebrew. Guide and companion to Tobit.

## Salomé
Stepdaughter of King Herod who, when offered anything she wanted by the King as a prize for her magnificent dancing, asked for John the Baptist's head on a platter.

## Samson
Champion promised to the Israelites to save them from the Philistines. Betrayed by both his wife and then Delilah, who gave away the secret that his massive strength was dependent on the length of his hair. Captured, blinded and shorn. When his hair grew back he pulled a whole building down, killing himself and many Philistines.

## Samuel
Prophet who anointed both Saul and David.

## Saul
First King of Israel who lost God's favour and grew jealous of his protégé, David.

## St Sebastian
Martyred with arrows while tied to a tree in 288. He accordingly became patron saint of pin-makers, archers and soldiers.

## Shadrach
Companion of Daniel in Babylonian captivity.

## Queen of Sheba
Balkis, Queen of the Sabaeans, modern day Yemen, who visited Solomon in Jerusalem 'with a very great train'.

## St Simeon Stylites, 390–459
Ascetic hermit, who spent 30 years up a 40 cubit pillar in Syria, inspiring other stylites in Syria, Egypt, Greece and Mesopotamia for the next 500 years.

## Solomon
Wise and wealthy King of Israel, to whom is attributed many of the Proverbs and the Song of Solomon. He began building the Great Temple in Jerusalem. He had 700 wives and 300 concubines. He was the son of David and Bathsheba and was famously visited by the Queen of Sheba. However, at the urging of some of his wives he built altars to foreign gods, causing God to split his kingdom in two after his death.

## St Stephen
(from Stephanos, Grk for crown or wreath) The Proto (or first) Christian martyr. Stoned to death for blasphemy in c 35AD 26th December.

## St Swithin
Bishop of Wincester who died in 862 and who chose to be buried in

the churchyard under the 'sweet rain of heaven'. When his successors tried to move his body inside after his canonisation on 15th July, it rained for 40 days.

St Teresa of Avila, 1515-1582
Reformed Carmelite Order, founded many convents and wrote on prayer. and strove for 'spiritual marriage' with Jesus. Canonised 1622.

St Theresa of Lisieux, 1873-97
'The Little Flower'. A Carmelite nun who died of tuberculosis after writing a moving autobiography. After several miraculous cures, she was canonised in 1925.

St Thomas, Doubting Thomas
Disciple and Apostle to India, who refused to believe in the risen Christ until he had seen him. Legend says on refusing his mission to convert India, Christ appeared and sold him as a slave to an Indian Prince who in due course he converted at Malabar. He was martyred at Mylapore (Madras). When Vasco da Gama arrived in 1498, he found a Christian community, the descendants of St. Thomas' converts.

St Thomas Aquinas, 1225-1274
Doctor Angelius. Influenced by Aristotle, and in his turn having a profound influence on the Catholic Church, he wrote many works, including Summa Theologica. He sought to emphasize the distinction between faith and reason.

Tyndale, William, 1494-1536
English translator of the Bible and Protestant martyr.

St Uriel
The leader of the Seraphim, whose name means God is my light, and who warned Noah of the flood and guarded the sepulchre of Jesus after the Resurrection.

St Ursula
5th century British Princess, massacred by the Huns at Cologne, along with her 11,000 virgin companions on pilgrimage to Rome. Undecimilla, the name of one virgin companion, may have been misread as undecim millia, 11,000, virgin companions.

St Valentine
A pagan Roman priest who, nevertheless, protected Christians, was converted in prison and clubbed to death in 290, despite curing the guard's daughter's blindness. Feast day 14th February.

St Veronica
Vera-icon, true likeness, as found on her head cloth on which Jesus wiped his face on the way to crucifixion.

St Walstan
The patron saint of farm labourers. A kind and pious Norfolk farm labourer who died in 1016.

Wesley, John, 1703-1791
Leader of the Methodist movement. *"I felt my heart strangely warmed. I felt I did trust in Christ, Christ alone for salvation; and an assurance was given me that He had taken away my sins, even mine, and saved me from the law of sin and death."*

Zacharias
John the Baptist's father, a priest, who did not believe the Angel Gabriel and so was made mute until John was born, as foretold.

Zadkiel
The Angel who appeared to Abraham to stop him sacrificing his son, Isaac.

Zophiel or Jophiel
The Angel who stood guard over the garden of Eden with a flaming sword after the expulsion of Adam and Eve.

Zwingli, Ulrich, 1484-1531
Swiss low church Reformer, who claimed that the bread and wine in communion remain completely symbolic.

**Abelites**

A 4th century North African sect that maintained total celibacy. (Abelites because they presumed Abel was a virgin as he had no children.) The sect was sustained through adoption.

**Absolution**

Forgiveness of sins.

**Aceldama**

The Field of Blood (Aramaic). The Potters' Field, which the chief priests and elders bought with the 30 pieces of silver Judas gave back to them, when he realised he had 'betrayed the innocent blood' of Jesus.

**Acephalites**

Originally a name given to headless monsters (from the Grk akephale, headless) and then to various Christian groups who rejected their kings, bishops, priests or ministers.

**Adamites**

Sects who either reject marriage, clothing or both.

**Adventists**

Christians who expect the Second Coming of Jesus soon – and/or a Golden Age afterwards.

**Advowson**

Ltn: Advocatio, a summoning – the right of the manor or bishop to award a church benefice.

**Agape**

Grk: Love.
Early Christians called their 'Love Feast', held after Communion, Agape. Poor Christians were invited and fed at the expense of the richer Christians.

**Agapetae**

The 'spiritual wives' of monks – condemned in the 4th century as potentially improper.

**Agnoitae**

Heretics who claimed that God was not totally omniscient, and other heretics who insisted that Jesus' humanity limited his omniscience.

**Agnostic**

Grk:Gnosis, knowledge
Definition of those who don't know, coined by T.H. Huxley in 1869, referring to the altar in Athens to the 'Unknown God', mentioned by St Paul.

**Agnus Dei**

Lamb of God.

## Agony

From the Grk: agon, a contest. The Agony in the Garden was the mental struggle or contest Jesus had with himself before embarking on the course of events that led to the crucifixion.

## Agonistes

From the Grk: Champion, like Samson.

## Albigenses

Or Albigensians or Bulgarians or Buggers or Cathars or Cathari; Virulently anti-clerical Manichean heretics from 12th and 13th century Northern Italy and Southern France, first persecuted in Albi in France. Pope Innocent III declared a crusade against them in 1208, but some survived until the 1390s.

## Almoner

One tenth of a monastery's income was distributed to the poor in alms by the almoner. From the Grk: eleemosyre, compassion.

## Alleluiah or Hallelujah

Hebrew- 'Hallelu Jah! Or Praise God!'

## All Souls' Day

2nd November, day appointed by Odilo, Abbot of Cluny, in 998 for the benefit of the 'Faithful Departed' and especially those souls in Purgatory.

## Altar

Ltn: altus, high.
The table used for religious sacrifice. The Christian communion table.

## Amen

Hebrew – truly. So be it.

## Amish

Followers of Jacob Ammann, the ultra-conservative Mennonite. Settled in Pennsylvania in 1714. They still speak German and avoid many modern 'Vanities'.

## Anabaptist

The name originally given to German Protestants in the 16th century, who insisted on adult re-baptism, ana meaning again, and then those many who disapproved of infant baptism or 'baptism before understanding'.

## Anathema

From the Grk: a thing set or hung up. An offering to the Gods. Evolved in Catholic and Calvinistic churches to mean a thing devoted to evil and became an even more severe form of solemn ecclesiastical condemnation than excommunication.

**Angels**
From the Grk: Angelus, messenger.
See page 106.

**The Angelic Hymn**
Luke 2. 14. Sung by the Angels
that appeared to the Shepherds of
Bethlehem, "*Glory to God in the
Highest.*"

**The Angelus**
Roman Catholic prayer, recited at
6 in the morning, 12 noon and 6
at night, at the sound of the
Angelus bell, to celebrate the
Annunciation.

**Anno Domini**
In the year of Our Lord – AD.
Practice initiated by the 6th
century monk, Dionysius Exigius.

**Annunciation**
The announcement by the Angel
Gabriel to the Virgin Mary that she
would be the mother of Christ.

**Apocalypse**
From the Grk: apocalypto, uncover,
a revelation
The Revelation of St John. The last
book of the New Testament.

**Apocrypha**
From the Grk: apokrupto, hide away.
The non-canonical books of the
Bible, often excluded from
Protestant Bibles.

**An Apostate**
From the Grk: Apo, from, and
statis, standing.
Someone who abandons their
religion.

**Aposteriori**
Ltn: from the latter.
In the context of Christianity,
concluding God exists from what
is good, godly.

**Apostle**
From the Grk: apostolos, one sent.
Applied to the Twelve Disciples of
Jesus and then Matthias, (chosen by
Lot to replace Judas) and Paul.
Listed with the Apostles' Creed on
page 103.

**The Apostles' Creed**
Creed said to be based upon the
doctrine of the Apostles, evolving
over the 2nd, 4th and 5th centuries
and reaching its present form in
the 11th century.
See page 103.

**Apostlic Fathers**
Christian writers who had been in
contact with the original Apostles.

**Apostlic Succession**
The doctrine that the mission given to the Apostles by Jesus in Matthew 28. 19, can only be maintained in an unbroken line; bishop succeeding properly consecrated bishop in line, and that only they can properly ordain clergy.

**Apotheosis**
From the Grk: apo, completion, and theos, God.
Deification, glorification, the finest example.

**Aramaic**
The Semitic languages of Aram, now Syria. The language spoken by Jesus and his Apostles.

**Arian**
Follower of Arius, denying Jesus' equality with the Father, his humanity and eternal pre-existence. Condemned as Heresy at the Council of Nicaea in 325.

**Armageddon**
The name in Revelations given to the battlefield of the final conflict between good and evil.

**Arminians**
Followers of Jacobus Hermansen or Arminius, who believed that all who repent and believe will receive forgiveness and eternal life.

**Augsburg Confession**
The declaration, or confession of faith put together by Melanchthon and Luther for Charles V at the Diet of Augsburg in 1530.

**Aureole**
From the Ltn: aura, air.
Full figure halo, often given to Jesus and the Saints.

**Ave Maria**
The smaller beads of the rosary, the larger being Pater Nosters, from the first two words of the Latin prayer to the Virgin Mary from Luke 1, 28.

**Avignon**
The site of the Papal Court from 1307 to 1377.

**The Athanasian Creed**
The Creed theoretically embodying the opinions of St Athanasius, that contains the Orthodox, Anglican and Catholic view on the nature of the Trinity.

**Banns (weddings)**
The publication three Sundays in a row in their parish church that a couple intend to get married.

**Baptism**
From the Grk: bapto, to wash.
The sacrament of purification and admission to the church, involving

washing or sprinkling with water in symbolic washing.

## Baptists
John Smythe set up a church in Amsterdam in 1609 from which was formed the General Baptists in London, in 1612, from which modern Baptists have evolved. Baptism by total immersion was only for adult believers, signifying acceptance by and of the Church.

## The St Bartholomew Day Massacre
The massacre of fifty thousand French Protestants, or Huguenots, in Paris and outside at the urging of Catherine de Medici, the mother of King Charles XI of France on 24th August, St Bartholomew's Day, 1572.

## Basilica
From the Grk: basilikos, royal. Originally palaces, then public Roman buildings with a nave and a space at one end for meetings or courts. Many were turned into churches with the rise of Christianity and many churches were modelled on basilicas.

## Basilian Monks
The Orthodox monastic order founded by St Basil in 360.

## Beatitudes
The eight blessings Jesus named at the start of the Sermon of the Mount.

## Behemoth
The Hebrew form of the Egyptian pehemout, water-ox, or hippopotamus, mentioned in the Book of Job.

## Bell, book and candle
Ceremonial excommunication: excommunication is declared, the Bible is closed (the Book of Life), the candle is put out by being thrown to the ground, (symbolic removal of the soul from the sight of God) and the bell is tolled, (signifying death).

## The Beloved Disciple
The disciple whom Jesus loved. Presumed to be St John, the author of St John's Gospel.

## Benedicte
Ltn: Bless you.

## Benefice
Possessions of the Church granted to people while they are living in compensation for their services; a 'Church Living'.

**Benefit of Clergy**
The privilege of English Clergy to be tried in a Church Court which would not impose the death penalty. Finally abolished in 1827.

**Bereans**
From the Bereans mentioned in Act 17, 10-11, who 'searched the scripture daily'. Followers of the Rev John Barclay, 1734-98, who left the Scottish Kirk in 1773 and insisted that all anyone can understand or know of God is in the Bible alone.

**Bible**
See page 108–109

**Bible Belt**
The religiously conservative Protestant Americans centred around the South and Central Mid-West.

**Bidding Prayer**
A Church of England prayer for the souls of benefactors before the sermon.

**Bishop**
From the Grk: episkopos, overseer. A senior cleric who oversees a diocese and can ordain or confirm.

**Blasphemy**
From the Grk: blasphemeein, to speak ill.

To speak or write contemptuously or disrespectfully of God.

**Bogomils**
Followers of the 10th century heretical Bulgarian priest, Bogomil, who denied the Trinity, claimed all flesh was evil and condemned the sacraments.

**Bohemian Brethren**
15th century Hussite sect in Prague which preceded the Moravians.

**The Book of Common Prayer**
The Anglican liturgy issued by Cramner in 1549. Revised and reissued in 1662.

**The Book of Kells**
8th century Latin copy of the Gospels, illustrated in Lindisfarne.

**Breviary**
The Book of the Ordinary and Daily Services of the Roman Catholic Church which it is the duty of clerics to recite, but not Eucharist, Marriage and other exceptional services, and therefore 'abbreviated'.

**Bull (papal)**
From the Ltn: bulla, seal.
An order proclaimed with papal authority and carrying the seal of the Pope.

## Calvary
The Latin word for the Greek word Golgotha, which is taken from the Hebrew word for skull, the name of the place where Jesus was crucified.

## Calvinists
Followers of the Protestant reformer John Calvin (1509-1564), who believed in predestination and rule by the congregation, with the Scriptures and the Holy Spirit as sole authority.

## Canon
A member of the cathedral chapter.

## The Canon
From the Ltn and Grk: canon, a carpenter's ruler.
The Books in the Bible which are accepted by most Christians. All the Books except those in the Apocrypha.

## Canonical Hours
See page 111.

## Canonization
The solemn confirmation by the Pope that a person, having already been beatified, is now a Saint and will be placed on 'The Canon', or accepted list of Saints.

## Capuchin
A particularly strict group of Franciscan Friars that separated in 1619. Their adoption of a pointed cowl called a Capuce gave rise to the name Capuchin.

## Cardinal
From Ltn: cardo, cardinis, a hinge on which things hang or depend. The senior 136 Roman Catholic Bishops who make up the College of Cardinals from whom the Pope is elected.

## Cardinal Virtues
Justice, Prudence, Temperance and Fortitude, from which all other virtues 'hang'. Faith, Hope and Charity are theological virtues.

## Carmelites
An order of begging friars founded in the 12th century and taking their name from Mount Carmel in Syria. Also known as the 'White Friars' for their white habits.

## Carol
From the Ltn: choraula, flute player.
Joyful hymns associated with the Nativity.

## Carthusians

An order of monks founded by St Bruno of Cologne who built the famous monastery in Chartreuse in 1084. Famous for the green alcoholic drink they invented, known as Chartreuse, and sold to maintain their Charterhouses.

## Catechism

From the Grk: Kateketichos, oral teacher.
Instruction by question and answer.

## Cathedral

The primary church of a diocese, which houses the Bishop's Throne or Cathedra.

## The Catholic Church

From the Grk: katholikos, comprehensive or universal.
A member of a Church which claims Apostolic Succession.

## Celibacy

From the Ltn: celibatus, unmarried. The requirement of some churches, particularly the Roman Catholic church, that only unmarried men be ordained into the priesthood. Not practised in the early church but recommended in the Councils of Elvira in 305 and Carthage in 390.

## Cenotaph

From the Grk: kenos, empty and taphos, tomb.
An empty or memorial tomb.

## Chalice

Eucharistic wine cup.

## Chancel

From the Ltn: can cellus, lattices. Originally a screen cutting the lawyers off from the public in Roman law courts. The east end of a church, containing the choir and altar, is the Chancel and is often separated from the congregation by a lattice screen.

## Chantry

An endowment to pay for the chanting of masses for the founder or benefactor of a church.

## Chapel

Originally the place where the small chest for the cloak or capella of St Martin was kept, known as the Chapelle by the Franks who revered it as an important relic. The word gradually came to be applied to small or private places of worship that were not large churches or cathedrals.

## Chapter

Cathedral community.

## Chasuble

From Ltn: casabula, little cottage. The sleeveless and often highly decorated over-garment worn by the priest while celebrating Mass, said to represent the seamless robe of Jesus.

## Chiliasts
From the Grk: chilias, a thousand. Millenarians who believe that at his Second Coming Christ will reign with his saints on Earth for a thousand years. Condemned as heresy in the late 4th century.

## Chrism
Consecrated oil for anointing in sacred rites.

## The Chrismon
The initial IHS (Ltn) and IHC (Grk) derived from the Greek spelling of Jesus. See IHS.

## Christian Science
The scientific system of divine healing, founded by Mrs Mary Baker Eddy in 1879 and expounded in her book 'Science and Health with a Key to the Scriptures', published in 1875.

## Church
From the Grk: kuriakon or kuriakos, belonging to the Lord. Both the building dedicated to Christian worship, and the Body of Christians themselves.

## Cistercians
A strict Benedictine monastic order famous for their farming, founded by Robert the Abbot of Molesme at Cistercium in 1098. Also known as the White or Grey Friars from their woollen habits.

## Clapham Sect
Group of Evangelicals led by the Abolitionist William Wilberforce in Clapham between 1790 and 1820.

## Clergy
From the Grk: kleros, inheritance or lot.
Holders of an allotted office; that of Christian minister.

## Collect
A prayer of a single sentence making one request.
*"Almighty God, unto whom all hearts be open, all desires known, and from whom no secrets are hid: Cleanse the thoughts of our hearts by the inspiration of thy Holy Spirit, that we may perfectly love thee, and worthily magnify thy Holy Name."*

## The Ten Commandments
Given to Moses on Mount Sinai by God for the Jewish People around 1250BC. See page 127.

## Compline
The final Canonical Hour (around 8pm), which completes the days' prayers.

## Concordat
A formal agreement between a Pope or Bishop and a Layman, Government or King.

## Congregationalist
Protestants who maintain that every congregation should independently direct its own affairs.

## Copt
From the Grk: aigyptos or Qibt, Egyptian.
Ancient Egyptian Monophysite Christians under the Patriarch of Alexandria.

## Counter-Reformation
The response by the Roman Catholic church, often seen as beginning with the Council of Trent in 1545 and ending with the 30 years war in 1618, to the emergence of 'reformed' or 'protesting' breakaway Protestant churches in the Reformation, through reform of its own affairs.

## Creed
From the Ltn: Credo, I believe.
Statement of belief.

## Crosier or Crozier
The Staff of a Bishop or Abbot topped with a crook. An Abbot carries his crook turned in on himself to suggest authority confined within his abbey or monastery, while a Bishop holds his crook outwards to signify his wider jurisdiction. An Abbot should veil his staff in the presence of a Bishop.

## Cross
Legend maintains that the cross of the crucifixion was made of cedar, cypress, olive and palm, representing the four quarters of the Earth. There are 14 principal Christian crosses. See illustration.

## Cyrillic Alphabet
Slavonic alphabet invented by St Cyril and his brother, c 850.

## De Profundis
Ltn: Out of the deep.
First words of Psalm 80 and part of the Roman Catholic burial service.

## Dean
From the Ltn: decanus, one set over 10 (canons).
The head of a Cathedral Chapter or College, formerly consisting of 10 canons.

## Deacon
In the early church, the person in charge of charity, now a cleric junior to a priest and bishop.

## Defender of the Faith
A title given to Henry VIII by

Pope Leo X in 1521 for his treatise attacking Luther. The letters FD have been on British coins referring to the monarch since the reign of George I.

## The Devil
From the Grk: diabolos, to slander or throw across.
The Supreme Spirit of Evil.

## Doctors of the Church
Saintly writers and teachers whose work advanced or clarified Christian thought and doctrine, and has been the subject of a proclamation by the Church. The Roman Catholic Church recognizes 33.

## The Four Latin Doctors
The four principal Doctors of the Western Catholic Church:
• St Augustine
• St Jerome
• St Ambrose
• St Gregory the Great

## The Four Greek Doctors
St Basil the Great
St Gregory Naziansen/the Theologian
St John Chrysostom
St Athanasius

## Domine, quo vadis
Ltn: "*Master, whither goest thou?*"
Peter's question to the dead Jesus when he appeared to Peter as he was fleeing persecution. To which Jesus replied "*I am going to Rome to be crucified again*," shaming Peter in to returning to Rome, where he was crucified.

## Dominions
The 6th of the 9 orders of Angels.

## Donatists
Heretical followers of Donatus, who insisted that mortal sinners be excluded from the church.

## Doxology
From the Grk: doxologia, hymn of praise to God.
The Greater Doxology, "Gloria in Excelcis Deo", is sung at communion. The Lesser Doxology, "Gloria Patria", is sung after each Psalm.

## Druses
Followers of Ismael ad-darazi. From Syria and Lebanon, whose faith is taken from the Bible and the Koran and who worship in both churches and mosques.

## Dunces
Followers of Duns Scotus, 1265–1308, from Dunse in Scotland, who ranted against innovation and new scholarship and came to be regarded as the enemies of progress, hence dunces, or idiots.

## Easter

The festival celebrating the Resurrection of Jesus. Held on the Sunday after the first full moon after the Spring Equinox. According to the Venerable Bede, the name came from Eastre, a goddess whose festival was celebrated at the Spring Equinox.

## Easter Eggs

Symbolizing life. Spring rent was often paid in eggs in rural communities.

## Ebionites

From the Hebrew ebion meaning poor. Ultra-Jewish Christians who split away from the non-Jewish church in 2nd century and not only rejected the Virgin birth but demanded the circumcision of all male Christians.

## Ecclesiastical

From the Grk: ekklesia, an assembly. In ancient Athens, where all male citizens over 20 could vote.
Applied by Biblical Commentators to the Jewish Commonwealth and then the Church. Relating to the church or clerics.

## Eden

From the Hebrew: Eden, delight. Paradise, Adam and Eve's garden.

## Emmanuel

Grk spelling of Hebrew: Immanuel, God with us.

## Epiphany

Grk: epiphaneia, manifestation, appearance.
Jesus' manifestation/appearance to the Gentiles through the three wise men of the East.

## Episcopacy

Church governed by Bishops.

## Epistle

Letter.

## Essenes

A Jewish religious community that advocated a simple and pious life from the 2nd century BC. Who may or may not have been in touch with John the Baptist.

## Eucharist

From the Grk: eucharistos, grateful. Communion. Jesus gave thanks at the last supper before giving his disciples bread and wine and so does the church during Holy Communion, Mass, the Lord's Supper. Eucharist is the name given to the service and the consecrated bread and wine of communion. Eucharist is recognized as a sacrament by most churches.

**Evangelist**
From the Grk: Eu, well or good, and Angellein, to bring news.
The bringers of good news. The writers of the four Gospels, Matthew, Mark, Luke and John.

**Excommunication**
Formal exclusion from the church community and the sacraments. See 'bell, book and candle'.

**Exorcism**
The expulsion of evil spirits.

**Extreme Unction**
'The Anointment of the Sick'. The anointing with oil on the brink of death as enjoined by James Ch 5, 14. One of the seven Catholic sacraments.

**Font**
From the Ltn: fons or fontis, fountain.
Bowl containing water for Baptism, often octagonal as are pulpits, representing the marriage of the divine (a circle) and the worldly (a square).

**Frankincense**
'Pure incense'. A fragrant gum originally from Arabia. One of the three gifts of the Magi to the infant Jesus, representing divinity.

**Fraticelli**
Little Brethren. Friars.

**Friars**
From the Ltn: frater, brother.
See list on page 110.

**The Religious Society of Friends, or Quakers**
Founded by George Fox who started preaching in 1647, condemning 'vanity' and 'frivolity' and insisting on charity and integrity. They reject oath-taking and violence and have no definite creed or hierarchy.

**Gehenna**
Literally the valley of Hinnam.
Where children were sacrificed as burnt offerings to Baal and Moloch.

**Gethsemane**
Literally, oil press. The Garden of Gethsemane where Jesus suffered was on the Mount of Olives.

**Gibeonite**
The enslaved 'hewers of wood and drawers of water' of the Israelites in The Book of Joshua.

**Gideon**
Son of Joash, to whom with his 300 men the Lord delivered the hosts of Midian.

## Gideons
An association of Christians who provide Bibles in hotel, hospital bedrooms and schools, founded in 1899.

## Gnostics
From the Grk: gnosis, knowledge. Early Christian sects who believed a special mystical knowledge would help them achieve salvation.

## Golden Calf
An idol made by Aaron and worshipped by the Israelites when Moses was on Mount Sinai, receiving the ten Commandments.

## Gospel
From the old English: god spell, good tidings.
The first four books of the New Testament.

## The Holy Grail
The cup or chalice used by Jesus at the Last Supper.

## Gregorian Calendar
The correction of the calendar introduced by Pope Gregory XIII in 1582 which had shifted 10 days in 1500 years. The Julian calendar made the year 11 minutes too long. Gregory commanded that the 5th October become the 15th October. The Gregorian Calendar was adopted in the UK in 1752 but not adopted in Russia until 1918.

## Gregorian Chant
Plainsong perfected by Gregory the Great.

## Hallelujah
Hebrew for Hallelu Jah, Praise Jehovah.

## Heaven
Old English: Heafen, God's home.

## Heptateuch
From the Grk: hepta, seven, and teuchos, tool or book.
The first seven books of the Bible.

## Heresy
From the Grk: heretos, choose, one who chooses (his own belief).
Belief that contradicts authorised Christian teaching.

## Hexameron
The six days of the Creation.

## Hip Hip Hooray
HIP is allegedly derived from the initials of Hierosolyma ist Perdita (Jerusalem is lost), and Hooray from 'Hu-raj' (to Paradise). Allegedly chanted by German knights, particularly when persecuting Jews.

## Hocus Pocus
A mocking mimicry of the words of consecration in the mass, hoc est corpus, used by non-Christian magicians in the East and gradually

adopted in the West.

## The Three Holy Hierarchs
St Basil
St Gregory Naziansen/The
Theologian
St John Chrysostom

## The Holy Ghost
Third person of the Trinity often
symbolized by a dove.

## The Seven Gifts of the Holy Ghost
Counsel
Fear of the Lord
Fortitude
Piety
Understanding
Wisdom
Knowledge

## To Sin against the Holy Ghost
Deliberately denouncing as evil
something which one knows to be
good.

## Hosanna
Hebrew: Save!

## Hospital
From the Ltn: hospes, a guest.
Initially lodgings for pilgrims,
which gradually became charitable
shelters for the sick.

## Hospitallers
The Knights Hospitallers (of St
John of Jerusalem, of Rhodes, of
Malta, being their successive
headquarters). An 11th century
military order which in the 18th
century turned back to tending the
sick and whose descendants
founded the St John's Ambulance
Association in 1877.

## Host
From hostia, a sacrifice.
The bread in communion.

## Huguenot
16th and 17th century French
Calvinists, who took their name
either from the German
eidgenossen, confederates, or from
the Gate of King Hugo at Tours
where Protestants used to meet.

## Hussites
Followers of the Bohemian, Jan
Huss (1369-1415), Dean of
Philosophy in Prague in 1401, who
promoted the Protestant ideas of
John Wyclif.

## Hypostatic Union
From Grk: hypo, under, and statis,
standing, hence the essence or
underpinning or basis.
The union of the Father, the Son
and the Holy Ghost in the Trinity
and the union of the divine and
the human in Christ.

## IHS

The Chrismon. The Latin form of the Greek IHC, derived from the Greek spelling of Jesus <u>IH</u>COY<u>C</u>. Also an acronym for "Iesus Hominum Salvator", Jesus Saviour of Man, "Iesus Habemus Socium", we have Jesus as our companion, "In Hoc Signio", by this sign (you shall conquer).

## Ichthus

Grk: fish.

This is an acronym of Jesus Christ Son of God Saviour: Jesus Christos Theo Uios Sater. One of the earliest Christian symbols, predating even the crucifix. Christian souls were often depicted as fish.

## Icon

Grk: eikon, image.

Religious pictures and objects of veneration in the Orthodox church, painted according to the Byzantine guide to painting.

## Iconoclasts

Image breakers, in particular opponents to sacred pictures.

## The Immaculate Conception

The Catholic dogma that the Virgin Mary was 'preserved immaculate from all original sin from the first moment of her conception'. This was declared an article of faith by Pope Pius IX in 1854.

## Immanuel

Hebrew: God with us.

## Indulgence

The forgiveness and cancellation of the earthly punishment due from a repentant sinner after the sacrament of penance has earned him forgiveness of his sin, and relief from spiritual punishment. Plenary indulgences remit all punishment. Partial indulgences remit some punishment, temporal indulgences remit punishment only for a time and there are also local, personal, perpetual and indefinite indulgences.

Pardoners were licensed to sell indulgences in the Middle Ages and it was the corrupt selling of indulgences in Germany that so incensed Luther and sparked his religious revolt.

## Infallibility

Dogma adopted by the Vatican Council in 1870 that the Pope when speaking ex cathedra, from his throne, or on religion or morality 'is free from error'.

## Inquisition

The department within the Catholic church that prosecuted heretics from c 1230, allowed to use torture from 1252. The Congregation of the Inquisition became the Court of Appeal in heresy trials. In 1908 the name was changed to the Holy Office.

## INRI
Letters nailed to the top of Jesus' Cross, standing for 'Iesus Nazarenus Rex Iudaerum', Jesus of Nazareth, King of the Jews.

## Interdict
A papal punishment involving the restriction of sacraments, placed on individuals, districts, communities or even countries.

## Jansenists
Followers of Cornelius Jansen (1585-1638), Bishop of Ypres, who were suppressed in 1713. They stressed the importance of original sin and predestination.

## Jehovah
When Moses asked God's name, God replied "*I am that I am*", written 'JHVH' (YHWH). The Jews regarded God's name as so holy that it should not be uttered. Next to the Hebrew consonants JHVH the Hebrew word for God, scholars wrote the vowels from the Hebrew word for Lord, ADONAI, suggesting that the word Lord be used instead of the word God. Over time these became muddled and matched. The consonents and vowels being put together and the name for God was taken to be Jehovah or Yahweh, J and Y and V and W being interchangeable.

## Jehovah's Witnesses
Founded by Charles Taze Russell in Philadelphia in 1872, and called the International Bible Students until 1931. Recognizing Jehovah as God, they believe that saluting a national flag and military service compromise his authority. They regard Jesus as God's champion on Earth and the perfect man.

## Jesse Tree
Jesus' family tree, proving his descent from David and David's father, Jesse.

## Jesuits
Members of the Society of Jesus, founded by Ignatius Loyola in 1534, to counter the Reformation and spread Christianity. Through its efficiency, discretion and ruthlessness, it began to be regarded as a threat and was eventually suppressed by the Pope in 1773, but then revived in 1814.

## Jubilate
Ltn: cry aloud.
The first word of Psalms LXVI and XC.

**Kyrie Eleison**
Grk: Lord have mercy.
The response at the beginning of communion.

**Lateran**
The palace of the Roman Laterani family, given to St Sylvester by the Emperor Constantine. The official residence of the Pope until the move to Avignon in 1309.

**Lateran Councils**
Five oecumenical councils. Councils whose conclusions theoretically applied to all Christians.

**Lateran Treaty**
Treaty in 1929 which established the Vatican City as a sovereign state within the nation of Italy.

**Latitudinarians**
Term of contempt applied to Anglican clergy after the English Civil War, who were relaxed about doctrine and ritual in religion.

**Lauds**
Morning prayer, using the laudate, "praise ye", over and over again.

**Lent**
From the old English lencten, spring, the time of the lengthening of days.
From Ash Wednesday to Easter.

Originally 36 days, but was fixed at 40 days in the 7th century to correspond to Jesus' fast in the wilderness.

**Limbo**
From the Ltn: limbus, hem or border. The edge or hem of hell for souls who had not acquired redemption through no fault of their own.

**Litany**
A prayer of supplication.

**Lollards**
From the Dutch: lollard, mumbler. Followers of John Wyclif, (1320-84) who disapproved of the wealth of the church, of bishops, clerical celibacy, indulgences and transubstantiation.

**The Long Cross**
Originally used in church service books to remind the priest when to make the sign of the Cross. Now generally used to suggest referral to a note. Also called the dagger.

**Lutherans**
Protestant Christian followers of Luther who insisted that worship be conducted in the local language, that the rule of the Scriptures were absolute and that, though tainted by original sin, faith in Christ

enabled people to be deemed
righteous by God.

## Magi
Ltn: wise men.

## Manna
The food provided by God to the
starving Israelites as they made
their way from Egypt to Israel.
Possibly a corruption of man-hu,
meaning what is it, or of mennu,
the Egyptian word for the gue
from the tamarisk.

## Manichaeans
Followers of the Persian Manni
(215-75), who believed that the
universe was divided and
controlled by good and evil in
constant conflict. The Manichaeans
believed the disciples and Apostles
had distorted Christ's message.
Manni was denounced as a heretic
and put to death in 275.

## Mardi Gras
From the French: Fat Tuesday.
Shrove Tuesday, the last day before
Lent.

## Martyr
From Grk for witness, testifier.
One who bears witness by his
death.

## The 7 joys, The 7 sorrows, The 7 Corporal works and The 7 Spiritual works of Mary
See Mary Mother of Jesus page 123.

## Mass
From the Ltn: misa, dismissal.
The Catholic name for
communion or eucharist. Because
the unbaptised were dismissed
before the eucharist began and the
rest of the congregation dismissed
at the end.

## The Massacre of the Innocents
The murder of boy babies under
the age of 2, ordered by Herod the
Great, to kill the future King of the
Jews, Jesus.

## Mendicant Orders
See Friars.

## Mennonites
Followers of Simon Menno, 1492-
1561, a Friesland Parish Priest, who
became an Anabaptist in 1536.
They refuse public office, military
service, clergy and infant baptism.

## Messiah
From Hebrew: mashiach, one
anointed.
The prophesised leader of the Jews,
who was to deliver them from
their enemies and reign forever.
Christians believe this was Jesus.

## Methodists

Originally John Wesley's Holy Club of Anglicans in Oxford set up in 1729, who observed rigorous method in their lives and worship. Became a separate church at his death in 1791. Evolved, split and eventually reunited with the Methodist Church of Great Britain in 1932.

## Metropolitan

A Bishop who controls a province and its suffragans, (ie the Anglican Archbishops of York and Canterbury).

## Millenarians, or Chiliasts

Believed Christ would return to Earth with the saints and reign for a 1000 years. Mille is the Latin and chilio is the Greek for 1000.

## Millerites

Followers of William Miller of Massachusetts, 1782-1849, who evolved into the Seventh Day Adventists.

## Miserere

Mercy.
The 51$^{st}$ Psalm begins "*Miserere me, Dei*", Have mercy upon me, Oh God.

## Mitre

From Grk and Ltn: mitre, head wrap.
Bishop's hat signifying the tongues of fire that descended upon the Apostles at Pentecost.

## Molinism

Followers of Louis Molina, 1535-1600, the Spanish Jesuit who taught that grace is given to all but must be accepted or consented to by the recipient to be effective.

## Monk

From the Ltn: monachus, a loner. A male member of a monastic community who has devoted his life to God.

## Monophysites

From the Grk: monos, one, and phusis, nature.
The belief that Jesus had one nature, a combination of divine and human, as body and soul are combined in man. Regarded as heretics by Catholics and Orthodox.

## Moravians

Descendants of the Bohemian Brethren, a Protestant sect emphasising simplicity and integrity.

## Mormons, or The Latter Day Saints

Adherents to the Book of Mormon or 'Golden Bible'. Joseph Smith 1805-1844 founded his church based on the Book of Mormon in the State of New York in 1830. When he was killed by a mob his place was taken by Brigham Young, 1801-1877, who led the church to

Salt Lake Valley, 1500 miles away, now called Utah, where they settled in 1847. Mormons revere the Bible as well as the Book of Mormon, believe in Baptism, Communion, the physical resurrection of the dead and the Second Advent, when Christ will come again and will rule the world from Utah. Until the US Supreme Court ruled against it in 1890, they practised polygamy.

The Morning Star of Reformation
John Wyclif.

Nestorians
Followers of Nestorius, Patriarch of Constantinople from 428 to 31, who taught that Christ had a holy and a human nature. He was condemned by the Pope in 430, nevertheless, his church spread through Asia.

New Testament
From the Ltn: testamentum, testament. In Greek the word is diatheke, which means covenant. Just as the people of Israel had a covenant with Jehovah, the life and death of Jesus established a new covenant, which is recorded in 27 books, and a complement to the Scriptures in the Old Testament.

The Council of Nicaea
The first oecumenical (world-wide) Council of the church called by Constantine the Great in 325 at Nicaea in Bithynia, to deal with the Arian heresy.

The Nicene Creed
Short statement of faith issued in 325 at the Council of Nicaea to combat the Arian heresy. Used in communion and baptism of Catholics, Orthodox and Anglicans.

Nimbus
Ltn: a cloud
Halo around head.

Nonconformist
Member of Protestant churches in Britain who do not conform with the doctrines of the Church of England.

Novena
From the Ltn: novenus, 9 each. Roman Catholic prayer for something or someone over 9 days.

Nunc Dimittis
The song of Simeon in Luke, *"Lord now lettest thou thy servant depart in peace"*, when he takes the child Jesus in his arms in the temple and recognizes him as the Messiah.

## Oecumenical Councils

From the Grk: oikoumenikos, the whole inhabited world.
Councils recognized by all Christians.

## Oecumenical Movement

The movement for the reunification of all churches.

## Old Believers

Members of the Russian Orthodox church who repudiated patriarch Nikos' liturgical reforms. Excommunicated in 1667.

## Old Testament

The first 39 books of the Bible, inherited by the Christians from the Jews.

## Oratorians

From the Ltn: oratorium, place of prayer.
A fellowship started in Rome by St Philip Neri in 1550s, making use of oratorios, sacred stories or dramas, to celebrate the Christian message.

## Holy Orders

The orders or ranks of the church. In the Church of England these are Bishop, Priest and Deacon, the Roman Catholics also have sub-Deacons.

## The Orthodox Church

The Holy Orthodox Catholic Apostolic Eastern Church. Complete separation from the Western Catholic Church was effected in 1054, the final arguments being over the Filioque controversy: Whether the Holy Ghost 'proceeded' from the 'Father only' or the 'Father and the Son'.

## The Oxford Movement

High church Anglican revival sparked in Oxford by the Catholic Emancipation Act of 1829 and fears that Catholic-minded Anglicans might actually become Roman Catholic.

## Pagan

Ltn: paganus, rustic.
Non-Christian, because pagan practices and beliefs lasted in the countryside long after they had vanished in towns. Paganus was also a contemptuous Imperial Roman word for a civilian.

## Palmer

A pilgrim from the Holy Land, who carried back a consecrated palm branch and laid it on the altar of his local church.

## Pandemonium

From the Ltn: pan demonium, all the demons.
Milton's City of Demons in Hell.

**Paraclete**
From the Grk: para kalein, to call to.
The Holy Ghost, the Advocate.
One called to aid, support, help or
comfort another.

**Paradise**
Persian for garden or enclosed
pleasure ground. Heaven.

**Pasch**
Easter. From the Hebrew Pesach,
Passover.

**Paschal Lamb**
The lamb sacrificed and eaten at
the Jewish Passover.

**The Passion**
Jesus' suffering.

**Patriarch**
From the Grk: patria, family,
arkhes, ruling:
> Abraham, Isaac, Jacob, the 12
> sons of Jacob and their
> forefathers.
> In the Western Catholic Church
> the Archbishops of Lisbon and
> Venice.
> The Orthodox Bishops of
> Constantinople, Alexandria,
> Antioch and Jerusalem.
> The Founders of Religious
> Orders (St Benedict, etc).

**Pelagians**
Followers of Pelagius. The British
monk who argued against the
importance of Original Sin.

**Pentateuch**
The first 5 books of the Bible.

**Pentecost**
From the Grk: pentecoste, fiftieth.
Whit Sunday. The Jewish Festival,
the $50^{th}$ day after the $2^{nd}$ day of
the Passover. The time when the
early Christians received the gift of
tongues at the 3RD hour, (9am).

**Pentecostal Churches**
Fundamental Protestant churches
who believe they receive the gift of
speaking in tongues.

**Persecutions**
See time line.

**The 5 Articles of Perth, 1618**
Imposed on the church by James
VI of Scotland:
> Kneeling at communion
> Observation of Christmas, Good
> Friday and Pentecost
> Confession
> Communion for the Dying
> Baptism of Infants

Ratified by the Scottish parliament
in 1621. Condemned by the
General Assembly at Glasgow in
1638.

Pharisees
From the Hebrew: Perusim, from Perash, separate. Those set apart. From 130 BC the Pharisees tried to promote government in accordance with the Torah, the first 5 books of the Old Testament.

Philistines
People of Philistia in Palestine.

Pieta
From the Ltn: pietas, filial and parental love.
Representations of Mary holding Jesus' dead body.

Pilgrims
From the Ltn: peregrinus, stranger or foreigner.
A traveller to a Holy Place.

Plymouth Brethren
Very low church, evangelical Christians founded in Ireland in 1828 by J.N. Darby, an Anglican priest. First English centre set up in Plymouth in 1830.

Pontiff
From the Ltn: pons, pontis, a bridge. The Pope, formerly any bishop. One in charge of the bridges. Priests in the Roman Empire had responsibility for bridges, headed by the Pontifex Maximus.

The Pope
From the Grk: pappas, father. The Bishop of Rome and the Head of the Roman Catholic Church.

Predestination
The Protestant belief that because God knows everything, he already knows who is saved or damned and therefore that our salvation or damnation is pre-determined.

Presbyterians
From the Grk: presbuteros, elder. Calvinistic churches ruled by elders.

Prime
From the Ltn: primus, the first. The first canonical hour, 6am.

Profane
Ltn: profano, outside the temple. Originally meaning non-religious, the word gradually evolved into meaning disrespectful, contemptuous of or anti-religion.

Propaganda
From propagate, to multiply. The Congregation of the Propaganda is a committee of cardinals set up by Pope Gregory XV in 1622 for propagating the Catholic Faith.

**Protestant**
A church not in communion with Rome or Constantinople. From the Lutherian protest against the recess of the Diet of Spires in 1529.

**Protomartyr**
The first martyr, St Stephen.

**Psalms**
From psallo, the twang of a harp string. Songs sung to a harp.
There are 150 songs in the book of Psalms, 73 allegedly by David, 12 by Asaph, 11 by the sons of Korah and 1 by Moses.

**Publicans**
In the New Testament, Roman tax collectors.

**Purgatory**
Place or condition in which some Christians believe souls are purified or purged from venial sin after death.

**Quakers**
See The Religious Society of Friends.

**Quarantine**
From the Ltn: quaranta, forty.
In the early church, penance lasting for 40 days, then the 40 day period in which those suspected of being infected with a disease were forced to wait outside harbour before entering port.

**Recessional**
The music and/or words said or sung or played when the priest and choir leave the service.

**Recusants**
From the Ltn: recusari, to refuse.
Those who refused to attend Church of England services, the last fine for which was imposed in England in 1782.

**Redemption**
From red, back and emere, to buy, to be bought back from.
In the Christian context, to be saved.

**Redemptionists**
Christians who bought back Christian slaves from Muslims.

**The Reformation**
The 16th century religious revolution which attempted to reform the corrupt practices of the Western Church, led by Luther, Calvin and Zwingli, from which the Protestant churches emerged.

**Requiem**
From the Ltn word: requiem, rest, hence requiem mass.
The first word of the mass of the dead.

## Reverend

From the Ltn: revereri, from vereri, to fear. Admire or respect deeply. Archbishops are formally entitled the Most Reverend, Bishops the Right Reverend, Deans the Very Reverend, Arch-Deacons the Venerable and all other clergy the Reverend.

## Rogation Days

From the Ltn: rogare, to ask. The three days before Ascension Day, when prayers are recited in procession.

## Roman Catholic

The Protestant name for the Western Church.

## Rood

From old English, rood, a cross. A cross or crucifix, hence the rood screen which separated the choir from the nave and was topped with a cross.

## Rosary

From the Ltn: rosarium, rose garden or garland. Loop of beads used by Catholics for the recitation of prayers. Allegedly introduced by St Dominic in the 13$^{th}$ century. The full rosary consists of 15 decades of Hail Marys, (small beads) each preceded by an Our Father, (large bead), and followed by a Glory Be to the Father, (large bead). Modern rosaries now normally consist of just 5 decades, known as a chaplet, or one third of a full rosary.

## Sabaoth

Hebrew for armies or hosts. Lord God of Sabaoth means Lord God of hosts/armies.

## Sabbath

From the Hebrew: Shabath, rest. The day of rest, 7$^{th}$ day of the week in the 4th commandment, commemorating the 7$^{th}$ day on which the Creation had been completed.

## Sabbattical Year

The one year in 7 when Mosaic Law insists that land lie fallow.

## Sacco Benedetto

Spanish: blessed cloak. The yellow cloak worn by those going to the stake to be burnt after condemnation by the Spanish Inquisition. Burnt because the church could not shed blood; as fighting bishops were required to use maces rather than swords.

## Sacrament

Ltn: sacramentum, the sacred oath taken by Roman soldiers not to desert their standards or commanders or turn their backs on the enemy. Christian Sacraments are sacred mysteries.

*An outward and visible sign of an inward and spiritual grace.* Definition in Book of Common Prayer.
Most Protestant churches recognize at least two sacraments:
• Baptism
• Communion
Catholics also recognize:
• Confirmation
• Confession
• Ordination
• Marriage
• Extreme Unction

## Sadducees

A Jewish group named after King Solomon's high priest, Zadok, who championed the upper classes in Israel and were fiercely opposed to the Pharisees. They denied the existence of angels and spirits, the resurrection of the body and punishment in the afterlife. They were strict followers of the Jewish written law. They were wiped out during the destruction of Jerusalem in 70AD.

## Sanhedrin

From the Grk: syn, together, hedra, seat.
The highest court of the Jews until the destruction of Jerusalem in 70AD, consisting of 70 priests and elders and a president.

## Sanctus Bell

The bell rung during the most sacred parts of communion.

## Saint

Title originally applied to Apostles, Evangelists, Martyrs and early Christians of great virtue. In 1170 Pope Alexander III insisted only the papacy could confirm sainthood.

## Salvation Army

A Christian organization that evolved from the Christian Mission in Whitechapel run by a Methodist minister called William Booth, 1829-1912. He formally declared it the Salvation Army and himself the 'General' in 1878 with the motto 'Through Blood and Fire' and the mission to help the poor. It rapidly spread across the globe.

## Samaritans

Inhabitants of Samaria in Palestine, who only accepted the first five books of the Bible as Holy Scripture and accepted only Moses as a prophet. Accordingly, they were looked on as inferior by other Jews.

## Sangrail

The Holy Grail.

## Satan

Hebrew, the enemy.
The Devil.

Scallop Shell
The emblem of St James of
Compostella and pilgrims generally
because pilgrims used to carry the
shells to scoop water out of
streams.

Scribes
Jewish lawyers in the New
Testament.

See
From the Ltn: sedes, seat.
The town where a bishop has his
throne and from where he takes his
title, not his diocese, which is the
territory he oversees.

Septuagint
Ltn: septuagintus, seventy.
The most respected Greek version
of the Old Testament and
apocrypha. Said to be translated
from the Hebrew by 72 Jewish
scholars in 72 days in the 3rd
century for the library in
Alexandria. It is often referred to
with the Latin numeral for 70,
LXX.

The Holy Sepulchre
The cave outside the walls of old
Jerusalem where Jesus' body was
lain after his crucifixion.

The Seraphic Blessing
The blessing of St Francis of Assisi
taken from Numbers 6. 24.

The Seraphic Hymn
The Sanctus, holy, holy, holy, sung
by Seraphim in Isiah 6, 3.

Seraphim
From the Hebrew seraph, a snake,
from the burning bite.
The highest of the nine choirs of
angels.

Seventh Day Adventists
Adventists, who take Saturday as
their Sabbath, abstain from alcohol
and tobacco and are strict followers
of the Bible. They took their name
in 1860.

Seven Deadly, Mortal or Capital
Sins
See page 126.

Shakers
Followers of Jane and James
Wardley of Manchester, who left
the Quakers in 1747. Ann Lee
took them to America, where they
practised celibacy and temperance.

Shamrock
Leaf used by St Patrick to explain
the Trinity.

Shibboleth
The word, meaning ear of wheat,
the Ephraimites could not
pronounce when challenged at the
Jordon crossings.

**Simony**
The trafficking of sacred things.

**Sinecure**
From the Ltn: sine cura, without care.
The perks and pay of a living/benefice without the duties/work.

**Southcottians**
Followers of Joanna Southcott, who died aged 64 in 1814. She declared herself the woman clothed in the sun in Revelations.

**Stations of the Cross**
See page 115.

**Stigmata**
Grk: stigma, the brand for marking slaves and criminals.
The psychological phenomenon in which some or all of the wounds of Christ appear on people.

**Stylites**
Pillar Saints. Ascetics who lived on top of tall pillars.

**Suffragan**
From the Ltn: suffrago, the ankle bone of a horse used by Romans as a voting slip.
An auxillary bishop, without formal oversight of a diocese but with a vote – from the duty of bishops to attend Synods and give their suffrage or vote.

**Swedenborgians**
Followers of Emmanuel Swedenborg, who set up the New Jerusalem Church in England in 1787. He wrote in Latin and claimed to have already seen the Last Judgement and be in contact with the spiritual world.

**Synod**
From the Grk: synodos, a meeting.
An assembly of clergy.

**Synoptic Gospels**
From the Grk: synopsis, seeing together.
The three Gospels of Matthew, Mark and Luke whose accounts of the life of Jesus and his teaching follow the same pattern, in comparison with the Gospel of John.

**Tabernacle**
From the Ltn: tabernaculum, tent.
The shrine the Jews carried with them while wandering in the wilderness. Divided into the Holy Place and the Holy of Holies, containing the Ark of the Covenant. In Roman Catholic church the tabernacle is the box containing the sacramental vessels.

## Te Deum
The first words of St Ambrose's Latin hymn, "*We Praise Thee, O God*", which he sang while baptising St Augustine in 386.

## Templars
The Knights Templar. So called because of their headquarters on the site of the Temple of Solomon in Jerusalem. Founded in 1119 by 9 French knights who took monastic vows and swore to defend pilgrims. In time, through their courage, commitment and integrity, and international network, they became enormously powerful and rich and were accordingly suppressed in 1312.

## Tertiaries
The third Holy Order. Sworn lay people who assisted friars, monks and nuns.

## Tetragrammaton
The four letter Jewish word for God, JHWH.

## Teutonic Knights
A military order which evolved from the German hospital at the siege of Acre in 1190, becoming an order in 1198, reserved for the nobility. The Teutonic Knights conquered and converted Prussia but were crushed by the Poles and Lithuanians at the Battle of Tannenberg in 1410.

## Thaumaturgus
Grk: wonder worker.
Worker of miracles.

## Theotokos
Grk: God bearer.
The Virgin Mary.

## Tithes
Originally voluntary gift of $1/10^{th}$ of production of land or income to the church, as Abraham gave one tenth of everything to King Melchizedek, a priest, after he had given him bread and wine. At various times and places, made compulsory.

## The Torah
Hebrew: the law.
The first five books of the Old Testament.

## Transubstantiation
The change of the substance of the bread and wine during Communion to the body and blood of Christ. Leaving their physical form or 'accidents' looking the same.

## Trappists
The Cistercians of the Abbey at Soligny la Trappe, who accepted the Strict Observance in 1892: the observance of silence and austere communal living.

## The Trinity
The three persons in one God, God the Father, God the Son, God the Holy Ghost, (see the Athanasian Creed). The word "Triad" was first used by Theophilus of Antioch around 180. "Trinity" was first used by Tertullian in 217.

## Unitarians
Christians who claim God is one person only and do not believe in the Trinity.

## United Reformed Church
The Church formed in 1972 by the unification of the Congregational Church of England and Wales and the English Presbyterian Church.

## The Vatican
The palace of the Pope, on the hill where the vaticinators, or soothsayers of ancient Rome, were based.

## Venerable
Ltn: venerabilis, worthy of honour. One who has achieved the first of three degrees of Catholic canonisation.

## Venial Sin
Ltn: venia, pardon or forgiveness. Sins that are forgivable and do not deny the sinner divine grace.

## Vespers
Ltn: verperos, evening. The sixth canonical hour.

## Vestry
Ltn: vestiarium, robing room.

## Via Dolorosa
Ltn: Doloros Way. Jesus' route from the place of judgement to his crucifixion, marked by the Stations of the Cross.

## Viaticum
Ltn: provision for a journey. Communion for the dying.

## Vicar
Ltn: vicarius, substitute. Originally the parson of a parish holding office as a substitute for a monastery or bishop and accordingly receiving a proportion of the tithes. Now an Anglican Parish Priest.

## The Vistation
The Virgin Mary's visit to her cousin Elizabeth, before the birth of John the Baptist.

## The 7 Virtues
See page 126.

## The Vulgate
The Latin translation of the Bible undertaken by St Jerome between 384 and 404, which was the first standard Latin text.

## Wesleyans
Followers of John Wesley who split from the Church of England in 1795.

## Wycliffite
A Lollard. They rejected monasteries, bishops and the Pope. Demanded scriptures in their own language and that only the godly should have power and property.

## XP
The Chi Rho.
XP stands for Christ from XPICTOC, the Greek word for Christos, Christ.
Chrysoun, the Greek for gold, starts with the same two letters and XP was stamped on coins centuries before Christ, as proof they were gold.
The Emperor Constantine had a vision of the Chi Rho with the words, "by this sign you will conquer" in 312, and Jesus visited him in a dream and told him to put it on his standards, before the Battle of Milvian Bridge.
Constantine did so and defeated the Emperor Maxentius despite massive disparity of numbers.

Leading to the official sanction of Christianity.

## Zealots
Fanatical Jews who refused to accept Roman rule, founded by Judas of Gamala. The sect was also known as the Cananaeans.

## Zion
Hebrew: tsiyon, a hill.
The Chosen People, the Church, the Kingdom of Heaven.

## Apostles' Creed

| | |
|---|---|
| Peter | I believe in God, the Father Almighty, Maker of Heaven and Earth: |
| Andrew | And in Jesus Christ His only son our Lord, |
| James the Great | Who was conceived by the Holy Ghost, Born of the Virgin Mary, |
| John | Suffered under Pontius Pilate. Was crucified, dead and buried, |
| Thomas | He descended into hell; The third day he rose again from the dead; |
| James the Less | He ascended into heaven, and sitteth on the right hand of God the Father Almighty |
| Philip | From thence he shall come to Judge the quick and the dead. |
| Bartholomew | I believe in the Holy Ghost. |
| Matthew | The Holy Catholic Church, the Communion of Saints. |
| Simon | The Forgiveness of sins. |
| Jude | The Resurrection of the body. |
| Matthias | And the life everlasting. Amen. |

## II Corinthians 13. 14

The grace of our Lord Jesus Christ, and the love of God, and the fellowship of the Holy Ghost be with us all evermore. Amen.

## A Prayer of St Chrysostom

Almighty God, who has given us grace at this time with one accord to make our common supplications unto thee; and dost promise that when two or three are gathered together in thy Name thou wilt grant their requests: Fulfil now, O Lord, the desires and petitions of thy servants, as may be most expedient for them; granting us in this world knowledge of thy truth, and in the world to come life everlasting. Amen.

## Aaron's Blessing

Numbers 6. 24–27
The LORD bless thee, and keep thee:
The LORD make his face shine upon thee, and be gracious unto thee.
The LORD lift up his countenance upon thee, and give thee peace.

Mary's Prayer of Thanksgiving – The Magnificat
Luke 1. 46-55
. . . My soul doth magnify the Lord,
And my spirit hath rejoiced in God my Saviour.
For he hath regarded the low estate of his handmaiden: for, behold, from
henceforth all generations shall call me blessed.
For he that is mighty hath done to me great things; and holy is his name.
And his mercy is on them that fear him from generation to generation.
He hath shewed strength with his arm; he hath scattered the proud in the
imagination of their hearts.
He hath put down the mighty from their seats, and exalted them of low
degree.
He hath filled the hungry with good things; and the rich he hath sent
empty away.
He hath holpen his servant Israel, in remembrance of his mercy;
As he spake to our fathers, to Abraham, and to his seed for ever.

Simeon's Prayer at the Temple – The Nunc Dimittis
Luke 2. 29-35
Lord, now lettest thou thy servant depart in peace, according to thy word:
For mine eyes have seen thy salvation,
Which thou hast prepared before the face of all people;
A light to lighten the Gentiles, and the glory of thy people Israel.

The Prayer of Zacharias – The Benedictus
Luke 1. 68-79
Blessed be the Lord God of Israel; for he hath visited and redeemed his
people,
And hath raised up an horn of salvation for us in the house of his servant
David;
As he spake by the mouth of his holy prophets, which have been since the
world began:
That we should be saved from our enemies, and from the hand of all that
hate us;
To perform the mercy promised to our fathers, and to remember his holy
covenant;
The oath which he sware to our father Abraham,
That he would grant unto us, that we being delivered out of the hand of

our enemies might serve him without fear,
In holiness and righteousness before him, all the days of our life.
And thou, child, shalt be called the prophet of the Highest: for thou shalt go
before the face of the Lord to prepare his ways;
To give knowledge of salvation unto his people by the remission of their
sins,
Through the tender mercy of our God; whereby the dayspring from on
high hath visited us,
To give light to them that sit in darkness and in the shadow of death, to
guide our feet into the way of peace.

The Lord's Prayer
Luke 11. 2-4
And he said unto them, When ye pray, say, Our Father which art in heaven,
Hallowed be thy name. Thy kingdom come. Thy will be done, as in heaven,
so in earth.
Give us day by day our daily bread.
And forgive us our sins; for we also forgive every one that is indebted to us.
And lead us not into temptation; but deliver us from evil.

Matthew 6. 9-13
After this manner therefore pray ye: Our Father which art in heaven,
Hallowed be thy name.
Thy kingdom come. Thy will be done in earth, as it is in heaven.
Give us this day our daily bread.
And forgive us our debts, as we forgive our debtors.
And lead us not into temptation, but deliver us from evil: For thine is the
kingdom, and the power, and the glory, for ever. Amen.

The Prayer of Stephen as he is Martyred
Acts 7. 59-60
And they stoned Stephen, calling upon God, and saying, Lord Jesus, receive
my spirit.
And he kneeled down, and cried with a loud voice, Lord, lay not this sin to
their charge. And when he had said this, he fell asleep.

Divine messengers. The nine choirs of Angels are divided into three orders:

The Counsellors:
- Seraphim
- Cherubim
- Thrones.

The Governors or Rulers:
- Dominions
- Powers
- Virtues.

The Messengers:
- Principalities
- Archangels
- Angels

# SYMBOLIC ANIMALS

Bull – the symbol of St Luke, associated with sacrifice.

Crane – a symbol of vigilance.

Donkey – appearing in many biblical stories, legend has it that they were marked with a cross after bearing Jesus into Jerusalem. Symbol of humility.

Dove – symbol of the Holy Spirit.

Eagle – symbol of St John and divine inspiration – hence their use in Church lecterns.

Fish – symbol of Jesus (see Ichthus) and Christian souls.

Lamb – symbol of Jesus. God is compared to a shepherd throughout the bible and souls to sheep.

Lion – symbol of St Mark the Evangelist, associated with power and kingship.

Pelicans – symbol of Jesus' sacrifice as pelicans were believed to pierce their own breasts with their beaks to feed their young on their own blood.

Ravens – symbol of God's Providence, having fed Elijah, when he hid from King Ahab, and St Paul the Hermit. According to legend they were white when dispatched by Noah to find dry land – but turned black with shame at their failure to do so.

Robin – symbol of fidelity, having been stained by the blood of Christ trying to staunch his wounds on the cross.

Snake – symbol of the Devil or sin.

From the Grk: ta biblia, the books.
The Christian Scriptures of the
Old and New Testaments.

The Canonical Books of the Bible
were decided upon by Pope
Damasus in 382.

The Books of the Old Testament
have traditionally been divided as
follows:
The Law:
• Genesis
• Exodus
• Leviticus
• Numbers
• Deuteronomy

Historical Books:
• Joshua
• Judges
• Ruth
• I Samuel
• II Samuel
• I Kings
• II Kings
• I Chronicles
• II Chronicles
• Ezra
• Nehemiah
• Esther

Poetic Books:
• Job
• Psalms
• Proverbs

• Ecclesiastes
• Song of Solomon
• Lamentations

Major Prophets:
• Isaiah
• Jeremiah
• Ezekiel
• Daniel

Minor Prophets:
• Hosea
• Joel
• Amos
• Obadiah
• Jonah
• Micah
• Nahum
• Habakkuk
• Zephaniah
• Haggai
• Zechariah
• Malachi

New Testament is divided into:
The Gospels:
• Matthew
• Mark
• Luke
• John

The Acts of the Apostles

The Letters:
• Romans
• I Corinthians

- II Corinthians
- Galatians
- Ephesians
- Philippians
- Colossians
- I Thessalonians
- II Thessalonians
- I Timothy
- II Timothy
- Titus
- Philemon
- Hebrews
- James
- I Peter
- II Peter
- I John
- II John
- III John
- Jude

Prophesy:
- Revelations

The Books of the Apocrypha, the non-canonical books, are:
- I Esdras
- II Esdras
- Tobit
- Judith
- Additions to Esther
- Wisdom of Solomon
- Ecclesiasticus
- Baruch
- Part of the Epistle of Jeremiah
- The Song of the Three Holy Children
- The History of Susannah
- Bell and the Dragon
- The Prayer of Manasses
- I Maccabees
- II Maccabees

In order to establish a standard text, St Jerome translated the Bible into Latin between 384 and 404. This is known as the Vulgate. The first complete translation of the Vulgate into English is the Wyclif Bible of 1384. Tyndale's version came out in 1525 and 1535 and had a profound influence on the wording and cadence of subsequent English versions. The first Bible printed in England (Southwark 1587) and first entire English edition printed anywhere (Zurich 1535) was that of Miles Coverdale.

The Great Bible, a copy of which all parish churches had to own by law, was published in 1539, and championed by Archbishop Cramner. The Geneva Bible, published in Geneva in 1560, divided the Chapters into numbered verses. On the orders of James 1 of England, VI of Scotland, 47 scholars produced the King James' or 'Authorized' version of the Bible in 1611.

# FRIARS

Augustinians: Austin Friars
Founded in 1243, combination of several ascetical groups under the rule of
St Augustine. The only order of friars to be founded directly by the Pope.

Carmelites: White Friars
Of twelfth century origin , and taking their name from Mount Carmel in
Syria, where they were founded, the Carmelites had a particular devotion to
contemplative prayer. Their white mantle earned them the name White
Friars

Crutched Friars: Crossed Friars
From the Latin 'Cruciati', or crossed, because of the crosses on their staffs
and sown onto their habits. Given a constitution by Pope Alexander III in
1169, they were supressed in 1656.

Dominicans: Black Friars
Founded by St Dominic de Guzman in 1215, based on the rule of St
Augustine and noted for their black cloaks and scholarship.

Franciscans: Grey Friars
Founded by St Francis of Assisi in 1209. Emphasis on poverty and preaching
to the poor. Called Grey Friars because their simple habits had no colour.

Trinitarians: Red Friars
The Order of the Most Holy Trinity founded by St John of Matha and St
Felix of Valois in 1198 with a special emphasis on redeeming prisoners and
slaves.

Canonical Hours
The seven hours of the day at which services and prayers should be held, as David says in Psalm 164 "*seven times a day do I praise thee*".

Matins

Prime

Tierce

Sext

Nones

Vespers

Compline

Prime, Tierce, Sext and Nones are the 1st, 3rd, 6th and 9th hours of the day, counting from 6 in the morning.

Born in a stable in Bethlehem to Mary and his foster father, Joseph. His birth hailed as that of the Messiah by Angels.

Mary and Joseph took Jesus to the Temple for the ritual purification of Mary and the formal presentation of a new Jewish child.

Jesus recognized by Simeon and the prophetess Anna as the Messiah.

Jesus brought gifts by the Magi, or three Kings, after the presentation. Warned by an Angel of Herod's determination to exterminate any possible alternative 'King of the Jews' mentioned to him by the Magi, Mary and Joseph fled with Jesus to Egypt.

After the death of Herod, the Holy Family returned from Egypt and went to Nazareth.

Accidentally leaving Jesus behind after their visit to the Temple in Jerusalem for the feast of the Passover when Jesus was 12, they found him after 3 days disputing with the Rabbis.

Jesus visited John the Baptist in the desert to be baptized and the Spirit of God descended upon him like a dove and a voice from heaven said, "*This is my son, whom I love; with him I am well pleased.*"

Jesus went with St Peter, St John and St James to Mount Tabor in Galilee to pray. Jesus was 'transfigured'; "*the fashion of his countenance was altered, and his raiment was white and glistening*". Moses and Elijah appeared.

After travelling through the country preaching and performing miracles, Jesus entered Jerusalem on a young donkey and was greeted by crowds who spread palm branches and cloaks before him.

Jesus drove the money-changers from the Temple. (Roman money had to be converted into Jewish money for use in the Temple.)

Jesus and his disciples shared the Passover meal, the last supper, on which the Eucharist, mass or communion, is based, the principal act of Christian worship.

He gave thanks, broke bread and gave it to his disciples saying, "*Take eat; this is my body.*" And he took the cup, and gave thanks and gave it to them saying, "*Drink ye all of it: For this is my blood of the New Testament, which is shed for many, for the remission of sins.*"

Jesus washed the disciples' feet.

After supper Jesus went with his disciples to the garden of Gethsemane where he prayed to be spared the suffering to come.

Judas Iscariot, one of Jesus' disciples, arrived in the garden and identified Jesus to the soldiers he had with him by kissing him. Peter hacked off the ear of the slave of the High Priest but Jesus healed him.

Jesus was convicted of blasphemy by the Jewish authorities and was taken to Pontius Pilate, the Roman Prefect, for him to approve the execution. Finding no reason to condemn him, Pilate sent him to Herod. When Jesus refused to speak, Herod sent him back.

Pilate offered the crowd the choice of Jesus or Barabas. They demanded the crucifixion of Jesus.

Jesus was then flogged, crowned with thorns and beaten and mocked by soldiers.

Jesus carried his own cross beam to his crucifixion, helped part of the way by Simon of Cyrene.

Jesus was crucified at the Place of the Scull, Golgotha or Calvary, outside the walls of Jerusalem. "*Jesus of Nazareth, King of the Jews*" was written on the sign above the cross on the orders of Pontius of Pilate.

The soldiers gambled for Jesus' clothes. He was crucified between two thieves, one of whom asked Jesus to remember him and to whom Jesus promised paradise.

St John, The Virgin Mary and St Mary Magdalene were all present at the Crucifixion.

Jesus cried *"My God, my God, why have you forsaken me?"*, was given hyssop dipped in vinegar on a reed to drink and then died.

A soldier stabbed his side with a spear and blood and water came out.

Jesus was placed in Joseph of Arimathea's tomb.

The following morning Mary Magdalene and other women found Jesus' tomb empty and were told by a man or two men in bright white clothes that Jesus had risen from the dead. Jesus himself then appeared.

Jesus then appeared to his disciples without doubting Thomas and then a week later to Thomas.

Forty days after the Resurrection, Jesus led the disciples to Bethany where, having blessed them, he was lifted up out of their sight: The Ascension.

# THE STATIONS OF THE CROSS

The 14 principal ones are, (though some churches consider there to be over 30):

• Jesus condemned to be crucified;

• Jesus taking up the cross;

• Jesus falling under the weight of the cross (the first fall);

• Jesus meeting the Virgin Mary;

• Simon of Cyrene being forced to carry the cross, in place of Jesus;

• St Veronica wiping the face of Jesus (leaving an image of his face on the cloth);

• Jesus falling under the weight of the cross (the second fall);

• Jesus encountering the women of Jerusalem;

• Jesus falling under the weight of the cross (the third fall);

• Jesus being stripped of his clothes;

• The Crucifixion;

• The Death;

• The Deposition (Jesus' body being taken down from the cross);

• The Entombment.

# SOME COMMON VARIETIES OF THE CROSS

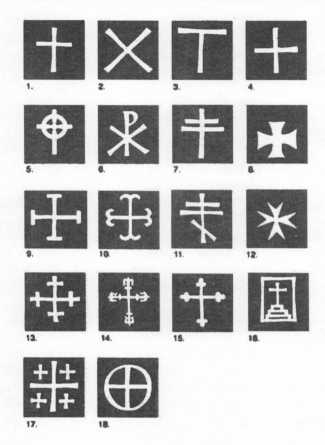

1. Latin
2. St. Andrews or Saltire
3. Tau or St. Anthony
4. Greek
5. Celtic
6. Chi Rho
7. Patriarchal
8. Patee
9. Potent
10. Moilne

11. Russian
12, Maltese
13. Crosslet
14. Fleury
15. Botannee
16. Calvary or graded
17.Jerusalem
18. Ring

## Miracles of Healing

The Nobleman's Son
John 4. 46-54

The Possessed man in the
Synagogue
Mark 1. 21-27; Luke 4. 33-37

Simon/Peter's mother-in-law
Matthew 8. 14-15; Mark 1. 29-31;
Luke 4. 38-39

The Sick at Sunset
Matthew 8. 16-17; Mark 1. 32-39;
Luke 4. 40-41

Curing of the Leper
Matthew 8. 1-4; Mark 1. 40-45;
Luke 5. 12-15

The paralysed man
20 *And when he saw their faith, he
said unto him, Man, thy sins are
forgiven thee.* Luke 5. 18-25

The Man at Bethesda
8 *Rise, take up thy bed, and walk.*
John 5. 1-17

The man with the withered hand
Matthew 12. 9-13; Mark 3. 1-6;
Luke 6. 6-11

Around Galilee
Matthew 4. 23-25; Matthew 9. 35

The Centurion's servant
Luke 7. 1-10
9 *For I am a man under authority,
having soldiers under me. and I say to
this man, Go, and he goeth; and to
another, Come, and he cometh; and to
my servant, Do this, and he doeth it.*
Matthew 8. 5-13

Raising of the widow's dead son
Luke 7. 11-17

Jesus heals a possessed man/two
men
Matthew 8. 28-34; Luke 8. 26-39
9 *My name is Legion. for we are
many.* Mark 5. 1-20

Raising of Jairus' daughter from
the dead and the healing of a
certain woman
Matthew 9. 18-25; Luke 8. 41-56
39 *And when he was come in, he saith
unto them, Why make ye this ado, and
weep? the damsel is not dead, but
sleepeth.* Mark 5. 22-42

The unclean woman
Matthew 9. 20-22; Mark 5. 24-34;
Luke 8. 43-48

The two Blind Men
Matthew 9. 27-31

Cured by touching his garment
Matthew 14. 34-36; Mark 6. 53-56

Sick in His own country
Mark 6. 1-6

The Gentile's daughter
Matthew 15. 21-28; Mark 7. 24-30

The deaf Man
Mark 7. 31-37

The multitude
Matthew 15. 29-31

The epileptic Boy
Matthew 17. 14-21; Mark 9. 14-29;
Luke 9. 37-42

The man born blind
*25 one thing I know, that, whereas I
was blind, now I see.* John 9.

The blind/dumb man
Matthew 12. 22-24; Luke 11. 14-
15

The blind man at Bethsaida
Mark 8. 22-26

The woman bowed together
Luke 13. 10-17

The man with Dropsy
Luke 14. 1-14

Lazarus raised from the dead
*25 I am the resurrection and the life:
he that believeth in me, though he were
dead, yet shall he live.* John 11. 1-45

The ten men with leprosy
*19 And he said unto him, Arise, go
thy way. Thy faith hath made thee
whole.* Luke 17. 11-19

The crowds in Judea
Matthew 19. 1-2

Bartimaeus
Matthew 20. 29-34; Luke 18. 35-
43

The blind & lame in the temple
Matthew 21. 14

High Priest's Servant's ear
Luke 22. 50-51

Other Miracles

The water into wine
*10 Every man at the beginning doth
set forth good wine; and when men
have well drunk, then that which is
worse. But thou hast kept the good
wine until now.* John 2. 1-11

The catch of fish
*5 And Simon answering said unto
him, Master, we have toiled all the
night, and have taken nothing.
nevertheless at thy word I will let down
the net.
6 And when they had this done, they
inclosed a great multitude of fishes. and
their net brake.* Luke 5. 1-11

The stilling of the storm
Mark 4. 37-41; Luke 8. 22-25
26 *And he saith unto them, Why are ye fearful, O ye of little faith? Then he arose, and rebuked the winds and the sea; and there was a great calm.* Matthew 8. 23-27

The feeding of the five thousand
Matthew 14. 15-21; Mark 6. 30-44; Luke 9. 12-17
9 *There is a lad here, which hath five barley loaves, and two small fishes. but what are they among so many?* John 6. 5-13

The walking on water
Mark 6. 48-51; John 6. 19-21
27 *But straightway Jesus spake unto them, saying, Be of good cheer; it is I; be not afraid.* Matthew 14. 25-31

The feeding of the 4000
Matthew 15. 32-39; Mark 8. 1-10

The money in the fish
Matthew 17. 27

The withering of the Fig Tree
Matthew 21. 18-22; Mark 11. 12-24

The second catch of fish
John 21. 1-14

The Resurrection

Matthew 28. 1-10; Mark 16; John 20;
36 *And as they spake, Jesus himself stood in the midst of them, and said unto them 'Peace be unto you.* Luke 24

The Salt of the Earth
Matthew 5. 13; Mark 9. 50; Luke
14. 34

The Lamp
Matthew 5. 14–16; Mark 4. 21;
Luke 8. 16, 11. 31

A City that is set on an hill
Matthew 5. 14

The Adversary and the Judge
Luke 12. 58; Matthew 5. 25

The Light of the Body
Matthew 6. 22 ; Luke 11. 34–36

The Friend of the Bridegroom
John 3. 28

The Fowls of the Air
Matthew 6. 26; Luke 12. 24

The Lilies of the Field
Matthew 6. 28–30; Luke 12. 2.

The Bread and Stone, Fish and
Serpent
Matthew 7. 9–11; Luke 11. 11–13

The Grapes and Thorns, Figs and
Thistles
Matthew 7. 16–20; Luke 6. 43–49

The House founded on Rock
Luke 6. 47–49
25 *And the rain descended, and the floods came, and the winds blew, and beat upon that house; and it fell not. for it was founded upon a rock.* Matthew 7. 24–27

The Two Debtors
Luke 7. 41–43

The Physician
Matthew 9. 12; Mark 2. 17;
Luke 5. 31

The Good Samaritan
31 *He passed by on the other side.*
Luke 10. 29–37

The Children of the Bride
Chamber
Matthew 9. 15; Mark 2. 18 ;
Luke 5. 34

The Importunate Friend
Luke 11. 5–8

The Cloth and the Wine
Matthew 9. 16; Mark 2. 21;
Luke 5. 36–39

The Children in the Marketplace
Matthew 11. 16–19; Luke 7. 31–35

The Divided Kingdom
Mark 3. 24–26; Luke 11. 17–20

The Strong Man's House
Matthew 12. 29; Mark 3. 27; Luke
11. 21

The Rich Soul
Luke 12. 16-21

The Watching Servants
Luke 12. 35-38; Mark 13. 33-37

The Cloud and the Wind
Luke 12. 54-56; Matthew 26. 2;
Mark 8. 11-13

The Empty House and the
Unclean Spirit
Matthew 12. 43-45; Luke 11. 24-26

The Barren Fig Tree
Luke 13. 6-9

The Shut Door
Luke 13. 24-30

The Sower and the Seeds
Matthew 13. 3-23; Luke 8. 5-15
*9 He that hath ears to hear, let him
hear.* Mark 4. 3-20

The Tares of the Field
Matthew 13. 24-30

The Mustard Seed
Matthew 13. 31-32; Mark 4. 30-32;
Luke 13. 18-19

The Leaven
Matthew 13. 33; Luke 13. 20-21

The Hidden treasure and Pearl of
great price
Matthew 13. 44-46

The Net
Matthew 13. 47-50

The Householder's Treasure
Matthew 13. 52

He Knoweth not how
Mark 4. 26-29

The Wicked Servant
Matthew 18. 23-35

The Shepherd, the Thief, and the
Door
John 10. 1-18

Labourers in the vineyard
*16 So the last shall be first, and the
first last. For many be called, but few
chosen.* Matthew 20. 1-16

The Wedding Guest
Luke 14. 7-11

The Great Supper
*21 Go out quickly into the streets and
lanes of the city, and bring in hither the
poor, and the maimed, and the halt,
and the blind.* Luke 14. 15-24

The Tower Builder and The
Warring King
Luke 14. 28-32

The Lost Sheep
Luke 15. 4–7

The Lost piece of Silver
Luke 15. 8–10

The Prodigal Son
*32 For this thy brother was dead, and is alive again; and was lost, and is found.* Luke 15. 11–32

The Unjust Steward
Luke 16. 1–12

The Rich Man and Lazarus
Luke 16. 19–31

The Two sons
Matthew 21. 28–32

The Master and Servant
Luke 17. 7–10

The Judge and the Widow
Luke 18. 1–8

The Pharisee and the Publican
*11 God, I thank thee, that I am not as other men are, extortioners, unjust, adulterers, or even as this publican.* Luke 18. 9–14

The Ten Pounds
*26 That unto every one which hath shall be given; and from him that hath not, even that he hath shall be taken away from him.* Luke 19. 11–27

The Wicked Husbandmen
Matthew 21. 33–41; Mark 12. 1–9; Luke 20. 9–16

The Porter
Mark 13. 33–37;

The Wedding Garment
*14 Many are called but few are chosen.* Matthew 22. 11–14

The Carcase and the Eagles
Matthew 24. 28; Luke 17. 37

The Fig Tree with the Tender Branch
Matthew 24. 32; Mark 13. 28; Luke 21. 29–31

The Good Man and the Faithful Servant
Matthew 24. 42–51.; Luke 12. 32–48

The Faithful Servant
Matthew. 24. 45–51; Luke 12. 42–46

The Foolish Virgins
Matthew 25. 1–13

The Sheep and the Goats
Matthew 25. 31–46

The Corn of Wheat
John 12. 24

In response to the reduction of the role of the Virgin Mary promoted by Protestantism, Catholics reemphasised her importance by using certain aspects of her life as objects for prayer and devotion. These include the following:

**The Seven Joys of Mary**
The Annunciation
The Visitation
The Nativity
The Epiphany
The Finding in the Temple
The Resurrection
The Ascension

**The Seven Sorrows of Mary**
Simeon's Prophesy
The Flight into Egypt
The Loss of the Holy Child
Meeting Jesus on the Way to Calvary
The Crucifixion
The Taking down from the Cross
The Entombment

**The Seven Corporal Works of Mary**
Tend the Sick
Feed the Hungry
Give Drink to the Thirsty
Clothe the Naked
Harbour the Stranger
Minister to Prisoners
Bury the Dead

**The Seven Spiritual Works of Mary**
Convert the Sinner
Instruct the Ignorant
Counsel those in Doubt
Comfort those in Sorrow
Bear Wrongs Patiently
Forgive Injuries
Pray for the Living and the Dead

# IMPORTANT PLANTS

Acacia – the burning bush through which God appeared to Moses (see also Bramble). Because it was not consumed by the flame, used to symbolize the immortality of the soul.

Almonds – Aaron's staff *"budded and brought forth buds, and bloomed blossoms, and yielded almonds"* to prove him God's choice of leader. Numbers 17. v.8.

Anemone – symbol of the Trinity.

Apple – traditionally, in the Western Church, the fruit of the forbidden Tree of the Knowledge of Good and Evil (malum is Latin for evil and apple). In the Eastern Church, using Greek not Latin, it is a fig, as Adam and Eve made their clothes out of fig leaves.

Aspen – the quivering leaves attributed to its use as the Cross at the Crucifixion (see also Palm, Cedar, Olive, Cypress and Holly).

Box – used to symbolize the Resurrection.

Bramble – a symbol of desolation and an alternative candidate for the burning bush.

Cedar – symbol of the faithful and is sometimes said to be one of four woods used in Jesus' cross, symbolizing all four quarters of the world.

Clover – symbol of the Trinity.

Columbine – symbol of the Holy Spirit, hence the name from the Latin, columba, dove.

Corn-ears – symbolize Holy Communion (through bread).

Cypress – sometimes said to be one of four woods used in Jesus' cross, symbolizing all four quarters of the world.

Dates – represent the faithful.

Elder tree – One of the trees on which Judas is supposed to have hanged himself (see also Fig and Judas tree).

Fig tree – One of the trees on which Judas is supposed to have hanged himself (see also Elder and Judas tree).

Grapes – the blood of Jesus (through wine).

Holly – according to legend the only tree that would allow itself to be used for the Cross – symbol of suffering and the Resurrection of Jesus.

Judas tree - One of the trees on which Judas is supposed to have hanged himself (see also Elder and Fig).

Lily – symbol of the Virgin Mary, the Church and purity.

Olive – symbol of peace. The leaf brought back to Noah by a dove to prove the waters were receding, and sometimes one of four woods used in Jesus' Cross to represent the four quarters of the world.

Palm – symbolizes victory. One of the four woods in the four-wood Cross, symbolizing the four quarters of the world.

Rose – symbol of incorruptibility – said to have no thorns until man tasted the fruit of the Tree of the Knowledge of Good and Evil.

Yew – symbol of death.

# THE SEVEN DEADLY, MORTAL OR CAPITAL SINS

Originally named by Gregory the Great in the 6th century.
Sins that deprive the soul of divine grace in order of importance:

• Pride

• Anger

• Lust

• Greed

• Envy

• Gluttony

• Sloth (originally sadness)

# THE SEVEN VIRTUES

Supernatural, Theological or Christian virtues:

• Faith

• Hope

• Charity

Cardinal or Natural virtues:

• Justice

• Fortitude

• Prudence

• Temperance

I am the LORD thy God, which have brought thee out of the land of Egypt, out of the house of bondage.

1 Thou shalt have no other gods before me.

2 Thou shalt not make unto thee any graven image, or any likeness of any thing that is in heaven above, or that is in the earth beneath, or that is in the water under the earth:

Thou shalt not bow down thyself to them, nor serve them: for I the LORD thy God am a jealous God, visiting the iniquity of the fathers upon the children unto the third and fourth generation of them that hate me;

And shewing mercy unto thousands of them that love me, and keep my commandments.

3 Thou shalt not take the name of the LORD thy God in vain; for the LORD will not hold him guiltless that taketh his name in vain.

4 Remember the sabbath day, to keep it holy.

Six days shalt thou labour, and do all thy work:

But the seventh day is the sabbath of the LORD thy God: in it thou shalt not do any work, thou, nor thy son, nor thy daughter, thy manservant, nor thy maidservant, nor thy cattle, nor thy stranger that is within thy gates:

For in six days the LORD made heaven and earth, the sea, and all that in them is, and rested the seventh day: wherefore the LORD blessed the sabbath day, and hallowed it.

5 Honour thy father and thy mother: that thy days may be long upon the land which the LORD thy God giveth thee.

6 Thou shalt not kill.

7 Thou shalt not commit adultery.

8 Thou shalt not steal.

9 Thou shalt not bear false witness against thy neighbour.

10 Thou shalt not covet thy neighbour's house, thou shalt not covet thy neighbour's wife, nor his manservant, nor his maidservant, nor his ox, nor his ass, nor any thing that is thy neighbour's.

ISBN 978-1-903071-37-3